Contents

List of Contributors

Yetta Goodman, Regents Professor at the University of Arizona is in the Department of Language, Reading and Culture in the College of Education. Yetta Goodman pioneered research on print awareness in young children studying children's early reading and writing in home and school settings to reveal their developing knowledge of written language and the nature of literacy development.

Janet Evans, formerly a primary school teacher, is Senior Lecturer in Education at Liverpool Hope University College. She is currently working as Literacy Consultant with the City of Liverpool on a two-year secondment. Janet has written five books on language and literacy for primary educators, and all of her articles on Early Years education, primary language and mathematics have been published. She has reviewed many books, videos and course materials for schools. Janet has taught in India and Nigeria and has been awarded two scholarships which allowed her to work and study in the USA. She has recently spent time in Australia researching literacy practices and has presented papers at international conferences in England and in the USA. Janet organises and teaches on many in-service conferences, but still manages to work in school doing action-based research.

Stuart Marriott was a primary school teacher in London before taking up his present post as Senior Lecturer in primary education at the University of Ulster. He is the author of three books and more than thirty articles about various aspects of primary education; his books include *Picture Books in the Primary Classroom* and *Read On: Using Fiction in the Primary School* (both Paul Chapman).

Judith Graham is Principal Lecturer in Education at Roehampton Institute, London. Her interests and teaching commitments are in all areas of literacy and children's literature. Her previous teaching has been in Inner London schools, at the Institute of Education and at the University of Greenwich. She is the author of *Pictures on the Page* (NATE, 1990) and also of *Cracking Good Books* (NATE, 1997).

Brenda Parkes was a lecturer at Griffiths University, Queensland, Australia where she lectured in language and literacy. She left in 1994 to take up freelance work and to write full time and she now spends 4–5 months each year in America and the remainder of the time in Australia. Brenda does a lot of keynote speeches at major conferences and she keeps up to date by working in school on a regular basis. She has written many language textbooks along with children's natural language, big books which are extremely popular internationally but particularly in England, America, Australia and New Zealand.

Pam Baddeley and **Chris Eddershaw** are both senior lecturers at Cheltenham and Gloucester College of Higher Education. They are the authors of *Not so simple picture books: Developing responses to literature with 4–12 year olds* (Trentham).

Liz Laycock is Principal Lecturer at the Roehampton Institute, London, where she was the Language teaching Studies Coordinator for many years. She is now the PGCE Primary programme convenor. She worked for many years as a primary teacher and Advisory teacher in London. She has contributed to several publications for the Centre for Language in Primary Education (CLPE). Most recently she is co-author of *Spelling and Phonics at KS1* and *Spelling and Phonics at KS2* (Scholastic – Curriculum Bank) and is a contributor to *Reading Under Control* (J. Graham and A. Kelly (eds.) Fulton). Her main interests lie in the areas of early literacy development, the assessment of literacy, children's literature and the development of English as an Additional Language.

Pat Hughes, is Senior Lecturer in Primary Education at Liverpool Hope University College. She has written on English History for Wayland, Heinemann, Folen, Scholastic and Hodder & Stoughton.

Geoff Fenwick is lecturer in the Department of Education and Community Studies, John Moores University, Liverpool. He has published a variety of books and articles in the field of children's books, and is a member of the International Society for Research in Children's Literature.

Kathy G. Short is an Associate Professor at the University of Arizona, where she developed a graduate programme in children's literature. **Gloria Kauffman** is an intermediate multi-age teacher (ages 9–11) in Tucson Unified School District, and has focused on inquiry and sign systems. **Cheri Anderson** is currently the co-ordinator of a programme in Visual Literacy for the Tucson Unified School District, where she works extensively with elementary teachers across the district.

Paul Johnson co-ordinates The Book Art Project from the Manchester Metropolitan University. The project has as its main aim the development of children's writing and visual communication through the book arts. His books on the subject include: *A Book of One's Own* (Hodder & Stoughton), *Literacy Through the Book Arts* (Heinemann, USA) and *Words and Images on the Page* (David Fulton). A book about children as illustrators, *Pictures and Words Together*, was published by Heinemann, USA in 1997. He contributed to the Longman Book Project and his articles have appeared in many educational journals on both sides of the Atlantic.

Anthony Browne went to Leeds College of Art where he did a degree in graphic design. He started his professional career as a medical artist at Manchester Royal Infirmary followed by fifteen years designing greetings cards for Gordon Fraser. His first book for children, *Through the Magic Mirror* was a real success and since then he has written and illustrated many books, each of which has his own inimitable style. Anthony Browne is now recognised internationally as one of the leaders of the picture book genre.

Foreword: the making of meaning through the picture book

Yetta Goodman

Whenever I listen to children read (usually as I am doing miscue analysis research), I am often drawn to the ways in which readers respond to illustration and I am intrigued with the ways different kinds of art in printed texts influence readers' construction of meaning.

I remember when my grandson Noah, age 6, was walking next to me through a crowded publishers exhibit with art forms of various kinds on the wall and hanging from the ceiling. Colleagues walking with me were as surprised as I was when Noah called out pointing to a picture without any words on the wall, 'Hey, grandma! Look there's Frida Kahlo, we were reading a book about her last week'.

. . . when Zeke, age 9 (not considered a strong reader), was reading one of the Magic School Bus books to me and he appropriately followed the written text across a two page spread under pictures of the school bus raising up and up and up.

. . . when Sara, age five, talked about the six different cats in a book we were reading together. The book had a single cat character according to my interpretation. 'Where are the six cats,' I asked. 'See,' she said and she showed me the different cats, each in a different pose, each somewhat different in shape, color and personality.

. . . when Antony, an inner city ten year old, was finishing the Three Billy Goats Gruff and came to the words in this version 'and he was so fat'. He folded back each page to check on whether the third billy goat was indeed fatter than the first two and said in a disbelieving tone, 'He ain't SO fat'.

Each of these episodes adds to my understandings about the influence of illustration in children's books and prompts me to ponder the role of illustration in the reader's construction of meaning.

Another experience that keeps me wondering about the nature of illustration is the way some illustrator/authors talk about how teachers minimize the role of illustration when they are teaching reading. They complain that teachers rarely follow childrens' leads when they excitedly attend to illustrations in the text. In fact, some report that they see teachers draw childrens' attention away from the art to focus on the written words.

The world we come to know as human beings is woven from shapes, images, smells, colors and feels. As we read we become aware of the trees waving in the breeze, of the smell of a storm brewing, of the feeling of snow and rain. Few experiences occur as separate experiences away from the integral nature of other sensuous experiences. And most are accompanied by language often oral but also written. It is therefore not surprising that books with words also include ranges of communication systems including illustration, diagrams, page edgings and many others.

Yet as teachers or teacher educators, we often ignore the multiple ways in which humans make sense of the world because of our concern about literacy development. We forget that few experiences involve any one isolated sense. We are often more concerned with how children are reading words rather than the depth to which they are responding to and making sense of a whole text including its illustrations, rhythms, its look and its feel as well as to the greater context in which the reading occurs. We take the art of the picture books as a way of knowing for granted. And as Stuart Marriott discusses in depth in this volume, we often relegate picture books as some stepping stone to motivate learning to read, and not as an integral part of the meaning making process.

Teachers need as much help as children to appreciate the importance of readers' responses to the art in books. Great art work by illustrators, photographers, calligraphers, graphic designers, painters and sculptors in picture books help readers extend and enhance experiences as they construct their meanings.

Adults are obviously aware of the significance of illustrated texts. Consider the huge market of travel books, cook books, art books, books on anatomy, books on fixing homes and cars filled with photographs, diagrams and pictures. Consider the kinds of social movements that are stimulated by the visual depiction of the plight of human beings. Consider the textbooks necessary to academic fields that support the construction of knowledge through a range of visual means in addition to written language. We listen carefully to the voices of authors as they sing their songs, explore their architecture, open up the rain forests and let us see the world through a system of meanings (sign or semiotic systems) that do not privilege written language as the sole source of communication. Often, however, little is done in classrooms or in teacher education programs to raise the intuitive responses of readers to conscious awareness in order to enhance their multiple ways of knowing by engaging the artwork in a text in the construction of knowledge and understandings.

As a number of the authors in this volume discuss, teachers are often so overly focused on teaching children to read that they forget that learning is taking in and interpreting the meanings of the whole, not just the print in books. They forget that the visual display that illustrators construct is significant to the communication between artists/authors and readers/viewers. Even the oral language conversations that are part of the responses to written texts add a semiotic dimension to the construction of texts.

As editor of *Whats in the Picture?*, Janet Evans provides the field of children's literature with a significant and useful volume that explores a diverse set of issues, theories and perspectives concerned with teaching and learning through the picture book. The authors of the different chapters explore the world of children's picture books in their own unique ways to capitalize on the importance of illustrations not as an add on but as integral to the meaning of every picture book. Each chapter brings to consciousness and makes visible the complexity of the special status of the picture book.

As Anthony Browne clearly states 'Making a picture book, for me, is not like writing a story then painting some pictures . . . No, it is more like planning a film, where each page is a scene that includes both words and images inextricably linked. What excites me . . . is working out the rhythm of the story and seeing how much is told by the pictures, how much by the words, and how much by the gap between the two.' (p. 194, this volume)

The authors in this volume provide teachers, teacher educators and readers of all ages with diverse perspectives, a range of classroom strategies and important issues to contemplate. Readers of this book have a rich set of articles to help them consider:

- The ways teachers use picture books to extend conscious awareness of art.
- The ways children use illustrations for making sense of the text.
- The multiple ways children of all ages are enabled to respond to pictorial texts.
- The use of picture books to enhance multicultural and English as a second language curricula.
- The use of picture books as inquiry into learning across the curriculum.
- The influence picture books have on children's morality, their cultural consciousness and their awareness of racism, sexism, and classism.
- The influence and use of picture books with older children and adults.
- The range of picture book genres: comics, non-fiction, picture books without words and other books with a diversity of artforms and styles.

Because the authors are well acquainted with children and picture books, the readers of the chapters will have a number of opportunities to hear the delightful language of children and teachers as they respond to and converse about picture books. And all the authors refer to their favourite children's books so that the reader ends up with an invaluable list of picture books for their own and their students' reading pleasure.

Each author in his or her own way presents the power of the picture book and reminds the reader that 'every text teaches what readers learn' (Meek, 1988). At the same time, they high-light the important role of the teacher in these encounters with illustrated texts. In addition, as the authors provide examples of how to use picture books with children, they emphasize the necessity of the readers/viewers constructing their own mean-ings based on their transactions with the text.

Although the focus of this book is the role of picture books for use with children, the information presented is as important to the enlightenment of the teacher as it is to the enchantment of the young reader. Hopefully with greater understanding about the power of the picture book, teachers and students of all ages will become more consciously aware of the unity of the experiences in our written world so that when we use the word 'reading' we always mean *reading the world* and never simply the word.

Introduction

Responding to illustrations in picture books

Janet Evans

The picture book, which appears to be the cosiest and most gentle of genres, actually produces the greatest social and aesthetic tensions in the whole field of children's literature.

(Egoff, 1981, p. 248)

We live in a world where everything in our daily ongoing life is constantly being challenged and changed. Resolute norms, values and beliefs which in the past, were rigorously held on to, are now threatened on a daily basis and, in relation to the education of young children, new initiatives move into and out of the limelight at an alarming rate. In trying to gain an understanding of the youth culture of today's western society, it is no longer applicable to say that young people from different cultural backgrounds are 'caught between two worlds'. *All* children have different societal and cultural backgrounds and *all*, at the end of the twentieth century are now 'caught' by many, hybridised worlds: the world of television, the world of advertising, computers, Coca Cola, roller blading, Bart Simpson, and the ever-changing social rules and values required by today's youth culture are but a few of the 'worlds' influencing the way children become acculturated into the society in which they live.

More than ever before people are beginning to see that they live in a 'postmodern' world: a world where society, culture and literature are in the process of challenging and changing life as it used to exist in the earlier parts of the twentieth century – the so-called age of 'modernism'. The postmodern society brings with it changes in the way people are able to make sense of texts, used in this sense to mean visual, dance, drama, music, song, media and IT as well as written texts. There has been an upsurge in the way readers have started to look at and relate to visual texts and the concept of visual literacy is now accepted as a way of trying to derive meaning from different types of texts. Kress and van Leeuwen (1996) consider these notions from a different point of view in their work looking at visual literacy from a grammatical perspective.

This whole period of change has meant a reappraisal of the way in which texts are now seen. Egoff, in the quote at the beginning of this introduction, clearly saw the picture book as having a part to play in this change and, as Fairclough (1989, p. 3) stated, 'writers on "postmodernism" have claimed that visual images are ousting language, and have referred to post-modern culture as "post-linguistic"'. This postmodern definition would certainly encompass the picture book genre where the illustrations need to be considered in part, if not in whole, to interact with and take meaning from the book. The reader does not really know what the writer intended . . . indeed does the writer? The writer's meaning may change and vacillate at each separate and therefore different reading, and even if we didn't understand what the writer intended does it really matter – the texts are for us to interpret depending on *who* we are, *where* we are, *what* we need from the text, consciously or subconsciously at any particular moment and *how* we relate to the text whilst interacting to the who, where and what mentioned above.

The meanings we attribute to texts are partly determined by the culture in which we have grown up. Factors such as race, gender and social class all have a part to play in forming our previous experiences and therefore in influencing the way in which we are able to make sense out of texts. In days gone by certain kinds of picture books for children were written almost to prescribed formulae, resulting in many traditional stories presenting certain ways of behaving as natural and appropriate for females and other ways of behaving as appropriate for males. These socially constructed texts almost inevitably had an effect on how readers responded to them and resulted in 'positioning' many readers in certain roles. Much postmodern fiction is concerned with exposing this contrived construction of texts and it is here that illustrations play just one of their many crucial roles. Out are the narrow,/stereotyped illustrations and in are the artfully crafted illustrations which carry much of the meaning in so many contemporary texts. It is the use of beautifully imaginative, thought-provoking and yet sometimes destabilising illustrations that has really seen the advent of many truly poly-semic picture books: texts that can be read and understood at different levels by readers of all ages from 4 year olds to 94 year olds. It is the multifaceted, multilayered nature of such literature that draws on a reader's previous world experience and knowl-edge of books. Styles (1996) asserts that polysemic picture books are arguably the ultimate postmodern text.

Illustrations have a crucial role to play in enabling children to gain meaning from books and, apart from in wordless texts, they work in partnership with print in picture books. Alongside the words, illustrations provide a starting point from which the reader gets meaning and to which the reader gives meaning. It was Louise Rosenblatt in the 1930s who, in her exploration of the relationship between the reader and the text, felt that any text was just a series of black marks on a page without a reader. The reader brings background information, previous experience and a whole range of sociocultural issues to the text which interact with the words to make them come alive. Rosenblatt (1938) called this type of interac-tion a 'transaction' and she used the term 'reader-response theory' to describe these interactions between the reader and the text.

The relationship between the reader and the text

Barthes (1977) took Rosenblatt's ideas one step further when he stated in his now famous article, 'The death of an author', that the meaning of a text is in the reader not the author and that 'the birth of the reader must be at the cost of the death of the author' (*ibid.*, p. 70). The author relinquishes his or her work to the readers and it is they who interpret the work in their own way according to what they bring to the text.

This may seem to indicate that the reader has the most important part to play and that the relationship is one sided. Not so! Don't let us forget Margaret Meek's ideas shared with us in *How Texts Teach what Readers Learn* (1988). In this distinguished little book Meek clearly and succinctly details how very often it is the text itself . . . the picture book . . . that is doing the teaching. Picture books must therefore be of the highest calibre and to deprive children of early and crucial interactions with quality picture books is potentially to do them a grave disservice in relation to their ability to learn how to respond to texts and therefore to read. Anthony Browne clearly relates to these sentiments because when asked (in this volume) what he felt about the many varied and diverse 'translations' that are made of his texts he replied, 'I deliberately make my books so that they are open to different interpretations, most of which I never hear about (probably just as well). Once a book is finished I have to let it go, like a child. What happens next is out of my control' (Browne, 1998, p. 195).

Responding to literature therefore involves a direct relationship between the reader and the text in a way that is personally meaningful to the reader. Young readers need to be given as many opportunities as possible to explore and respond to the myriad of excellent picture books which are now available. A reader-response approach to sharing texts usually entails children working collaboratively, initially working with teachers but usually moving on to working with peers. Chamber's *Tell Me* (1993) approach to discussing books can be used to get children talking freely about the book being considered and is seen as a non-threatening, non-aggressive approach to scaffolding children's responses to texts.

Chamber's work, encouraging children to respond to picture books is very much in tune with the work done by Short and Pierce (1990) on 'reader-response theory' and 'literature circles'. Kathy Short, inspired by the work of Rosenblatt, agrees that there is no one correct interpretation of a literary work, but multiple interpretations, each of them profoundly dependent on the prior experience brought to the text by each reader. Short felt that to enable children to analyse and to develop more sophisticated interpretations of books they must be able to share their personal responses. It is obvious that in order to provide children with the opportunity to talk about books in a social, collaborative setting, they need a format. Hence the notion of literature circles, whereby small groups of children read a book prior to responding to what the book is about. In this fashion children help each other to come to personal interpretations of the book. Daniels (1994), in his excellent book on literature circles, feels that giving children the opportunity to respond to books in this collaborative manner provides an ideal situation for teachers to scaffold children's learning. Indeed he feels that literature circles owe a lot to the concept of scaffolding: 'Literature circles are predictable, playful, and meaning centred activities in which kids exercise lots of choice and responsibility, children function at a higher level than they could unaided, and everyone gradually adopts a new language for talking about their work together' (*ibid.*, p. 37).

Children very often respond to picture books more effectively if they know how a text works and how the author/illustrator has constructed the text. Polysemic texts make use of intertext – that is, they make reference to other stories and they expect/presume the reader will be able relate to the intertextual references. Many authors and illustrators make use of intertext but some authors use it more than others. Janet and Allan Ahlberg (1978), in their book *Each Peach Pear Plum*, rely on their readers knowing about the well-known British traditional tales and rhymes which feature in the book. Without this knowledge readers couldn't fully respond to the text. John Prater in his ingenious text, *Once Upon a Time* (1993) plus the sequel *Once Upon a Picnic* (1996), relies almost entirely on the reader being able to relate to the intertextual references. All texts exist in relationship with other texts, some more obviously than others and, as Stephens and Watson (1994, p. 32), point out in their fascinating look at how secondary pupils can respond to the picture book genre, texts are 'linked to other texts by reminiscences, similarities, reworkings, generic affiliations, intellectual contexts, story patterns'. They point out that to make sense of a text, 'Readers . . . bring a wealth of associations to the text' (*ibid.*).

Authors and illustrators often make use of other strategies to draw the reader into the text and therefore respond to the story. They use the concept of 'gaps' where the reader has to use his or her imagination to interpret the words and the pictures together to make sense of the text. The inferences that the reader must make to fill the 'gaps' in the story and therefore get meaning that is not explicitly stated come from different sources: the reader's existing knowledge of story structure in terms of setting, plot, characterisation, theme, style and resolution; the reader's knowledge of intertext (already mentioned); the reader's knowledge of the syntax and grammar of how texts work; and the reader's knowledge of rhyme and alliteration in relation to certain texts. Thompson (1987, p. 123) describes these 'gaps' as 'spaces between sentences, chapters, events, details, characters, narrative viewpoints, textual perspectives and so on'. Whilst Iser

(1978, p. 169) states, 'Whenever the reader bridges the gaps, communication begins . . . the blanks leave open the connections between perspectives in the text, and so spur the reader into co-ordinating these perspectives – in other words, they induce the reader to perform basic operations within the text'.

Most children do learn to respond to texts and many of them are helped along the way through the discourse of illustrations in polysemic texts. The work of the contributors in this book documents many diverse and different ways in which children have been enabled to respond as readers to pictorial texts but perhaps it is the voice of a child, albeit a postmodern, somewhat surreal child speaking about her rather bizarre adventures in Wonderland who should have the first word:

> Alice was beginning to get very tired of sitting by her sister on the bank, and having nothing to do: once or twice she had peeped into the book her sister was reading, but it had no pictures or conversations in it, *'and what is the use of a book,'* thought Alice, *'without any pictures or conversation?'* (Carroll and Browne, 1988, p. 1, my emphasis).

Bibliography

Ahlberg, J. and Ahlberg, A. (1978) *Each Peach, Pear, Plum,* London: Viking Kestrel.

Barthes, R. (1977) *Image, Music, Text,* London: Fontana.

Browne, A. (1998) The Role of the Author/Artist, in J. Evans (ed.) *What's in the Picture: The Meaning of Illustrations in Picture Books,* London: Paul Chapman.

Carroll, L. and Browne, A. (1988) *Alice's Adventures in Wonderland,* London: Julia MacRae.

Chambers, A. (1993) *Tell Me: Children, Reading and Talk,* Stroud: Thimble Press.

Daniels, H. (1994) *Literature Circles: Voice and Choice in the Student Centred Classroom,* New York: Stenhouse.

Egoff, S. (1981) *Thursday's Child,* Chicago.

Fairclough, N. (1989) *Language and Power,* New York: Longman.

Iser, W. (1978) *The Act of Reading,* London: Routledge.

Kress, G.R. and van Leeuwen, T. (1996) *Reading Images: The Grammar of Graphic Design,* London: Routledge.

Meek, M. (1988) *How Texts Teach What Readers Learn,* Stroud: Thimble Press.

Prater, J. (1993) *Once Upon a Time,* London: Walker Books.

Prater, J. (1996) *Once Upon a Picnic,* London: Walker Books.

Rosenblatt, L. (1938) *Literature as Exploration,* New York: Appleton-Century.

Short, K. and Pierce, K. (1990) *Talking about Books,* Portsmouth, NH: Heinemann.

Stephens, J. and Watson, K. (1994) *From Picture Book to Literary Theory,* Sydney, NSW: St Clair Press.

Styles, M. (1996) Inside the tunnel: a radical kind of reading-picture books, pupils and post-modernism, in Watson, V. and Styles, M. (eds.) *Talking pictures: Pictorial Texts and Young Readers,* London: Hodder and Stoughton.

Thompson, J. (1987) *Understanding Teenagers' Reading,* London: Croom Helm/Methuen.

Chapter 1

Picture books and the moral imperative
Stuart Marriott

The next settlement was Erasmo, a village smaller than
Avellenada, but substantial enough to boast a sizeable school
building over whose doorway were inscribed the words Lectura –
locura. I asked the driver if he could translate, and after some
hesitations he found the words. 'Reading, lectura. Lectura, reading,' he said proudly.
   'And locura?'
   'Is madness, pardner.'

(Rushdie, 1995)

I am not entirely sure what Salman Rushdie means to convey in
this enigmatic little passage towards the end of a brilliant novel,
but perhaps it is a salutary reminder that the act of reading is not
always as innocuous and predictable as it appears but is sometimes uncertain, irrational or even threatening (and he should
know). Picture books have not yet given rise to any fatwa, as far
as I know, but they too are usually more complicated and occasionally more potent than they seem at first glance.

Multiple approaches

One perennial view of picture books is as an age-related form of
entertainment particularly appropriate for children before and
in the early stages of formal schooling. Such very young children are assumed to be capable of eager response to materials of

a wide variety of types and styles in which a story, however fragmentary, is sustained mainly or entirely through pictures. The question of how children learn to make sense of pictures or by what process they learn to respond to the narrative structure of picture books is not usually raised, or if it is the assumption tends to be that the development of such capacities is implicit in cognitive and emotional maturation and is thus unproblematic. It is also assumed that such maturation will eventually lead children away from picture books into what are regarded as more sophisticated or at least more elaborate entertainments; picture books, in this view, have little or no relevance for older children, and certainly none for adults.

These two ideas, that picture books are an age-related phenomenon and that the ability to understand pictures is an unambiguous skill which young children automatically develop, often lead to a third, that picture books provide a kind of prop which sustains and supports the initially incompetent beginning reader. More or less explicit within such accounts is the conviction that in time the crutches the picture book affords can be cast aside as the child's increasing expertise in decoding the printed word unaided enables him or her to dispense with them. And often implicit is the belief that the sooner that children's behaviour resembles that of the adult reader, seen as routinely and skilfully absorbing pages of unbroken and unillustrated print, the better.[1] This view is often held by older children themselves who resist picture books on the grounds that they are babyish. However, once again, such a perspective leaves a variety of questions unanswered and often unaddressed. By what mechanism, through what mental process, does illustration enable readers to comprehend the written word more competently? Do pictures truly support the efforts of the beginning reader or do they in fact, as Bettelheim and Zelan (1991) have argued, distract his or her attention from a proper concentration on decoding print? Does not the real reading behaviour of competent adults include texts which incorporate both words and pictures such as newspapers, magazines, advertisements, road signs, maps, plans and diagrams, as well as illustrated books about cookery or gardening or DIY or whatever (not to mention the huge numbers of picture books and comic books written specifically for older readers and adults)? If so what are the implications for the initial teaching of reading?

If these are relatively ingenuous or at least somewhat partial descriptions of the picture book form there exist in addition many much more subtle and comprehensive approaches, such as those of Meek (1988), Nodelman (1988), Graham (1990) and Lewis (1990). Quite often, however, these subsume what are genuinely stimulating and illuminating discussions of picture books within more general accounts of either written children's literature or of the visual arts; in other words they tend to see the picture book as a subspecies of the novel, or of painting, and to apply critical techniques accordingly. Thus, for example, in Landsberg's (1988) lengthy survey of children's literature, picture books are only very briefly discussed (in a chapter revealingly titled 'Books to encourage the beginning reader') as one genre within the totality of written fiction for children. In complete contrast, Doonan (1993) has developed accounts of the work of picture book authors which explore visual effects in great detail using a variety of critical concepts derived from the vocabulary of art criticism.

The point about these different views of the characteristics of picture books is that although they all have their limitations they are also all valid. Picture books are so wildly varied and diverse in format, style, subject matter and putative audience, so heterogeneous in their intertextuality, so eclectic in their reference to the structure and form of the novel and the short story, to painting and photography, to film and television and even in some cases to music and sculpture, that it is hardly surprising that they are also extraordinarily flexible and versatile in use. Thus they can legitimately be read and discussed as entertainment for babies, or as material for decoding practice, or as literary products, or as artistic compositions, or indeed in other ways. The genre is anything but self-contained and easily definable, as Lewis (1996, p. 6) has pointed out:

> In short, the picture book is a bit of a tart, it'll go with anyone and occasionally doesn't mind a bit of cross-dressing. It's perfectly at home with parody too – quite prepared to laugh at itself and at those genres which are a bit staid and set in their ways, like the traditional tale, the non-fiction book and the reading scheme book. It's happy to pull faces when cartooning but is also capable of supreme feats of decorousness and sometimes profundity.

Plurality and ideology

For present purposes two of the most significant attributes of picture books need to be addressed. In neither case are they unique to the genre and thus cannot be seen in isolation as defining the form but both seem to be indispensable; necessary but not sufficient attributes. The first of these is the peculiar relationship between words and pictures; picture books are inescapably plural. Defining this hybrid relationship precisely is not easy, and different commentators (Lewis, 1996) have resorted to a variety of metaphors: derived from music (counterpoint), from craft (weaving), from literary theory (irony) and even from geology (tectonic plates). However, whatever imagery is seen as helpful, in all cases the reader has by some means to take account of what are certain to be separable impressions given the different media involved, and the act of reading a picture book requires him or her to focus on the gap between what the words appear to say and what the pictures appear to say. To read a picture book, then, is to engage in a highly creative process by which the reader attempts to reconcile an inevitable tension, to connect the ostensibly disconnected, to integrate the apparently discontinuous. Picture book authors, of course, play with this tension incessantly; they may intend to use the pictures or the words to consolidate or enhance, or to modify or reconstruct, or indeed to challenge or contradict each other. In some cases the relationship may be left deliberately quite ambiguous and equivocal while in others it may be resolved by readers in a multiplicity of different ways.

The second important feature of picture books is that they are inherently ideological. In some ways the word is unfortunate since in common use it often implies disparagement but for present purposes it is used as a neutral term to refer to the network of beliefs, values and social practices which are explicitly espoused by or more often implicitly sustained within the text. In this sense all texts are ideological but especially texts intended for children. As Stephens (1992, p. 8) has asserted:

> children's fiction belongs firmly within the domain of cultural practices which exist for the purpose of socialising their target audience. Childhood is seen as the crucial formative period in the life of a human being, the time for basic education about the nature of the world, how to live in it, how to relate to other

people, what to believe, what and how to think – in general the intention is to render the world intelligible. Such ideas as these are neither essential or absolute in their constitution but are constructed within social practices, and the intelligibility which a society offers its children is a network of ideological positions, many of which are neither articulated nor recognised as being essentially ideological.

A good example of an ideological position taken within fiction for children and only relatively recently recognised is that of the pervasive sexism of stories in which patronising and patriarchal gender relationships are portrayed as normal and thus simply taken for granted. Such ideological assumptions were thoroughly explored some years ago in several studies, such as those of Dixon (1977) and Stones (1983), which provided detailed accounts of the prevalent and in such writers' views inappropriate sexist and sometimes racist implications of much children's literature, not only in the popular stories of authors like Enid Blyton and Roald Dahl but also in the work of much more highly regarded writers like Robert Westall, K.M. Peyton, Penelope Lively and Diana Wynne Jones. Similarly, Ursula Le Guin, quoted in Hunt (1994, p. 140), came to the conclusion that her acclaimed *Earthsea* trilogy of novels for children was inherently sexist and wrote a fourth volume to try to redress the balance herself. In the case of sexism, then, a variety of social and cultural changes led to a fairly sudden awareness by some writers, readers and critics of what until then had been more or less unacknowledged.

The moral imperative

Given the heterogeneity of picture books, their ideological assumptions are similarly multiple and complex but certainly they very frequently incorporate the concept of childhood as a period of transition from infant egocentricity to adult maturity. Since this process is perceived as both significant and developmental many if not all picture books provide perspectives on ethical and moral issues which reflect the author's perception of value and his or her aspirations for the present and future nature of social life. For present purposes this may be called the moral imperative: that is, consciously or unconsciously, overtly or covertly, picture books provide through the combination of images and words, themes and ideas, texts and subtexts, a representation not only of how the world is but also of how it ought to be.

An obvious example is the type of picture book which can be seen as a vehicle for the explicit advocacy of moral precepts, as a means of prescribing specific advice to impressionable young readers. This has a long history and indeed the roots of children's fiction as a whole lie partly in the religious didacticism of the nineteenth century. Overt finger-wagging exhortation is perhaps rarer nowadays and in several recent picture books like Brown and Krensky's *Perfect Pigs* (1983) and Ross's *Super Dooper Jezebel* (1988) the moral perfection of a leading character is seen as sufficient reason for him or her to come to a sticky end, but didacticism still flourishes in the rather neglected area of picture books which purport to provide sensible information and guidance to children about personal problems they may face in their progress to adulthood: illness, disability, bereavement, physical and sexual abuse, family breakdown, bullying, and similar issues (Gooderham, 1993). The titles of a few typical books provide an accurate indication of their flavour: *We Can Say No!* (Pithers and Greene, 1986); *When Uncle Bob Died* (Althea, 1982); *I Have Epilepsy* (Althea, 1987); *Living with Mum* (Storrie, 1989); *We're Going to Have a Baby* (De Saint Mars and Bloch, 1991); *Children Don't Divorce* (Stones, 1991); *Topsy and Tim Have Itchy Heads* (Adamson and Adamson, 1996). In passing it may be worth noting that if it is true that reading of any kind is above all an interactive process whereby the reader brings experience to, and in a sense negotiates with, the text, rather than one of passive and unquestioning absorption of whatever messages it contains, the faith of the authors of such books in the effectiveness of their sagacious (if somewhat relentlessly cheerful) advice may be misplaced.

Much more thoughtful and much more interesting are those picture books in which the appraisal of authentic and substantive issues is central but in which the moral imperative is to a greater extent implied or tacit rather than asserted. The range of concerns of such books includes the same individualistic and personal problems of family and peer relationships, but also encompasses questions of wider social and political interest such as race and gender, the environment and conservation, social and community conflict, war and peace, and even global inter-dependence. In relation to all such topics a range of picture books exists which provide not direct advice but a more subtle and sometimes provocative, yet often apparently naive and guileless, discourse.

The examples that follow are just that: examples drawn from the publications of three of the best-known, popular and very prolific picture book makers currently working in Britain, namely, David McKee, Michael Foreman and Anthony Browne. There are many more who are equally distinguished, even if the work of authors from other English-speaking countries is ex-cluded, let alone books published in other languages. However, even such a narrow focus can provide cases which exemplify my themes and arguments and since each of these authors has in different and idiosyncratic ways explored the boundaries of the picture book form they can also provide a flavour of the com-plex and sophisticated ways in which picture books function.

Problematic families

David McKee's *Not Now Bernard* (1980) is, at the simplest level, a story about a little boy who tries desperately but unavailingly to attract his parents' attention. Even when he is eaten by a mon-ster in the garden, their only response is to repeat the words of the title: ' "But I'm a monster," said the monster. "Not now, Bernard," said Bernard's mother.'

The text is simple and mantra-like in its repetition, and in the pictures the characters seem flat and two-dimensional within a bright, not to say garish, yet plain background, although highly significant details are included which function to link the pic-tures together. The overall effect is very funny: author and reader are engaged in a kind of conspiracy of mutual knowledge which excludes the parents. This simplicity and humour has led to substantial use of the book for early reading purposes with very young children (Moon, 1985) but it also raises issues which are rather more ambiguous. The behaviour of the parents as described in the pictures, especially after their son has seem-ingly been swallowed up by the monster, increasingly seems cold and aloof; but on the other hand Bernard's conduct is at best tactless (always addressing his parents at awkward

Not Now Bernard (McKee, 1980a)
Reprinted by permission of Anderson Press from D. McKee (1980a)
Not Now Bernard

moments) and that of the monster reprehensible (biting Bernard's
father's leg). The book thus has something to say about the ways in
which families work or in this case apparently do not work. One
group of 10–11-year-olds, for example, concluded that the book
illustrated the fact that mutual concern is the most important feature of the relationships between family members and not the
possession or absence of material goods. As they put it, 'caring's
about loving them and stuff' (Baddeley and Eddershaw, 1994, p.
45) and since Bernard although materially well provided for lacks
love, the family is dysfunctional. An alternative but not necessarily
contradictory account might point to the story as centred on the
theme of power and powerlessness within family relationships. In
such a reading the child Bernard attempts to assert his power, and
succeeds in trivial ways, but the real control and authority in this
(as in the reader's?) family is that of the adults: it is the mother who
turns the light out at the end of the book.[2]

The themes of McKee's *Who's a Clever Baby Then?* (1988) are
not dissimilar. Here Baby is left in Grandma's charge (mother
has rushed off looking harassed in the first picture and father is
nowhere to be seen). Grandma's ingeniously alliterative but

increasingly desperate attempts to elicit from Baby the names of the ten or eleven different animals they encounter is met by the stolid repetition of: ' "Dog," said Baby.' Finally they meet some dogs, to which Baby responds: ' "Cat," said Baby.' Once again, then, the theme is of the child's attempts to subvert the boundaries imposed by adults; intrinsic to Baby's responses are a recognition of the power of words, especially names, a refusal to play the game of language according to the rules devised by adults and an assertion of an alternative interpretation of reality. The title of the book is thus ironic rather than patronising: this baby really is clever. In an indirect way the pictures also reinforce the theme carried by the words: the social settings in which Baby and Grandma are portrayed are anarchic and disorganised rather than safe, secure and reassuring; a motley array of characters is shown engaged within their own disconnected and seemingly bizarre stories; and the disjunctive effect of these visual jokes is heightened by the partial replacement of normal rules of perspective with a more primitivist or child's-eye point of view. The pictures, then, as well as Baby's words, undermine Grandma's attempt to portray the world as regular, rule bound and predictable; there are more things in heaven and earth than are dreamt of in Grandma's philosophy.[3]

Anthony Browne's *Piggybook* (1986) is also about the transformation of everyday realities, both literally, like *Not Now Bernard* and metaphorically as in *Who's a Clever Baby Then?* The story is about the Piggott family. Mrs Piggott is treated by all the other family members as a servant and eventually departs leaving only a note: 'You are pigs.' Discovering that they are quite unable to look after themselves, on Mrs Piggott's return Mr Piggott and the boys plead with her to stay; subsequently household tasks are appropriately shared amongst the whole family. However, such a thumb-nail sketch of the plot omits nearly all that is interesting about the book. The title reminds us of the term piggyback and the front-cover picture of a woman carrying a large and cheerful man and two smiling boys on her back reinforces the impression, and may also prompt the phrase 'male chauvinist pigs'. The title page's pictures of flying pigs may remind us of yet another well-known saying. The brightly coloured pictures of Mr Piggott and the boys at the beginning of the story contrast with the sombre tints of the faceless Mrs

Piggott doing housework; she is working in an unknown, unrecognised netherworld. When she disappears not only are the male characters shown literally transformed into pigs but in a way very typical of Browne pigs' snouts also appear in extraordinary and unlikely places in the pictures. None of this is mentioned in the text, the only hint being that the characters who earlier called or demanded now snort or squeal or grunt. On Mrs Piggott's climactic return her shadow dramatically falls across a floor where Mr Piggott and the boys are rooting around for scraps in what now looks almost entirely like a pigsty, before the family is shown happily reconstituted. In this as in all his books, Browne expects his readers to bring their knowledge and their experience to the text and the pictures and to work hard at resolving their multiple and complex connections. Are there family situations so intolerable that the only solution is the abdication of responsibility, like that of Mrs Piggott? If so, is her return psychologically likely? And how does the optimism of the ending relate to the characteristics of this, and the reader's, family?[4]

In each of these three picture books the authors make use of the inherent flexibility of the connection between words and pictures to raise in the context of family relationships issues which are essentially moral. The degree of explicitness in the moral imperative varies; both of McKee's books are more open to a variety of interpretations than *Piggybook* which could be read as rather insistent on one particular point of view.[5]

Human and animal kindred

There are many more picture books exploring the dynamics of family life, but in some cases aspects of the family provide only one of the themes. Two of Anthony Browne's books provide excellent examples of the connections between behaviour and interaction within families and moral issues and questions of more extensive relevance. A central feature of both is Browne's proposal that the relationship between parents (especially fathers) and their children is analogous to the relationship between human beings and animals in captivity (especially the primates), and the way in which he uses each of these themes to reflect and extend the meaning of the other can readily be traced. Many thoughtful accounts of *Gorilla* (1983) already exist (such as by

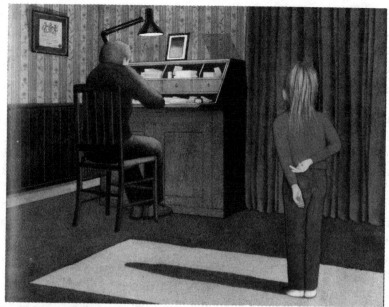

Gorilla (Browne, 1983)
© 1983 Anthony Browne; Reprinted by permission of the publisher Walker Books Ltd, London

Graham, 1990; Fox, 1996, and by Browne, 1994a himself) and so only a brief and focused discussion of this outstandingly accomplished and extraordinarily subtle picture book is necessary here. Several pictures encapsulate the gulf that exists between Hannah and her father. In the first the reader sees them at breakfast, distant from each other, not communicating; almost everything is depicted in regular geometric shapes comprising hard sharp lines and the colours are cold blues and whites and greys. On the following page Hannah is shown standing, again at a distance, watching her father working at a desk and seeming to ignore her. Her face cannot be seen, but her posture – tense, nervous and submissive – is painfully expressive.

Two pages later Hannah is seen in bed and the low angle from which the reader views the picture shows her seemingly imprisoned by the bars of the bedhead. Later in the book as Hannah gazes through the very similar bars of cages at a chimpanzee and at an orang-utan she, and the reader, can empathise with creatures in a predicament comparable to her own. Here Browne, whose texts are sometimes flat and colourless, provides the perfect, intensely evocative words to accompany the poignant pictures: 'She thought they were beautiful. But sad.' Each theme is eventually worked through to a happy ending: Hannah and the gorilla eat a meal together in which the picture – close contact between the two, soft curved textures, warm colours – is the antithesis of the breakfast earlier, dances with him in the moonlight and even kisses him, and the tension between Hannah and her father is resolved as he offers to take her to the zoo. However, the impact of the pictures of the caged animals remains with the reader long after the book is finished, and Browne himself seems to have felt a need to return to the theme several years later, in *Zoo* (1992).

Both the words and the pictures in *Zoo* contribute to the contrast that Browne builds between the sad defeated dignity of the animals and the conscious or unconscious vulgarity of the human beings (especially the ghastly father) observing them. At each opening the left-hand page consists of text and a fairly small picture of members of the family, usually squabbling or behaving offensively, while the right-hand page is a large and meticulous picture of one of the animals in its cage or pen, an increasingly disturbing series of images culminating in a detailed close-up of, once again, a gorilla. In these animal pictures Browne uses the physical features of the book to strengthen his point: the boundaries of the page itself reinforce the black border to the picture which in turn emphasises the bars or netting of the cage which constrains the animals. Although to the gross and ignorant father the zoo continues to represent merely an opportunity for the indulgence of some of the less attractive habitual characteristics of human beings, by the end of the book other members of the family begin to be disturbed: ' "I don't think the zoo really is for animals," said Mum. "I think it's for people." ' In the final opening on the left-hand side it is the child narrator of the story who is confined, both by the shadows of vertical bars and by a thick black boundary to the picture, while on the right-hand side the whole zoo is shown in silhouette under a huge and open night sky. The text says: 'That night I had a very strange dream. Do you think animals have dreams?'

Browne here raises some uncomfortable moral questions: who here is appropriately regarded as beastly? What evidence is there that we human beings are morally superior? Who really ought to be kept in cages? For what purpose and in what conditions can the routine incarceration of animals be justified?

Zoo (Browne, 1992)
Reprinted by permission of Random House.

The moral and the fabulous

All the picture books discussed so far are ones in which magical transformations of various kinds occur, but each is embedded in what are at least superficially authentic experiences and contexts of social and family life. Many other picture books depart radically from such nominal realism and some are completely disconnected from it. In each case, however, whatever form the characters take and in whatever situation they are placed the moral implications are pointed straight at the reader.

If the gorilla is a heroic, emblematic figure in many of Anthony Browne's books,[6] the dinosaur plays a similar role in

Foreman's *Dinosaurs and All That Rubbish* (1972) although here
the tone is animated, even breezy, and the humour less dark.[7] A
bowler-hatted businessman uses up the earth's resources for a
fruitless trip to another star, leaving nothing but rubbish and
waste behind. On his return he finds that in his absence re-
awakened dinosaurs have cleaned up the mess, and the earth is
once again the paradise it was before he ruined it. This time,
says a dinosaur:

> '. . . the earth belongs to everyone, not parts of it to certain
> people but all of it to everyone, to be enjoyed and cared for.'
>   'Yes EVERYONE!' sang the birds and the cats and the mice and
> the mammoths, the serpents, the dodos, and the apes.
>   'EVERYONE!' came the chorus from all living things.
>   'EVERYONE! EVERYONE!'

If the words seem a little too emphatic (even without the capital
letters), the lively watercolour pictures of jolly dinosaurs de-
stroying cars and breaking up roads have a playful quality
which defuses the reader's sense of ecological evangelism. The
same is true of *Panda's Puzzle* (1977), in which the eponymous
hero travels the world trying to find out whether he is a white
bear with black bits or a black bear with white bits, only to
conclude at the end of his journey that it doesn't really matter.
Although the moral of the story is rather obvious, the painterly
illustrations of exotic locations around the world provide in-
triguing diversions. But it is in *War and Peas* (1974) that a more
intricate dialogue between words and pictures is evident. The
animals in King Lion's country are starving; although his neighbour the greedy Fat King has plenty of food he not only refuses
to help but also launches an invasion. However, the Fat King's
soldiers are so obese and so slow that they are easily out-
manoeuvred by King Lion and his nimble colleagues, and as the
rain begins to fall the overweight tanks and trucks plough up
the land so that seeds will now grow. King Lion points out to the
defeated Fat King the immorality of supplying his already
bloated troops with yet more food while spurning the pleas of
the poor and hungry of other countries, but concludes:

> 'Peace,' said the Lion.
>   'No, no, no,' groaned the Fat King, 'don't mention peas, ever.'
>   'Peace,' repeated the Lion.
>   'Never heard of it,' said the Fat King. 'What's the recipe?'

As they approached the city they were much
impressed by the richness of everything.
"Surely they have more than they need," said
the Grocer hopefully.

War and Peas (Foreman, 1974)
Reprinted by permission of the author.

However, the pictures transform a fairly conventional moral fable
into something altogether more dynamic. Throughout the book
the scenery consists of food: mountains are cakes and fruit pies,
buildings are milk shakes and jars of biscuits, and the supply
trucks of the Fat King's army are loaded with tarts and puddings.

The power of this lies in the size and detail of the edible
background settings compared with the tiny protagonists, and
in the type of food depicted, all sweet and sickly children's party
food with lashings of cream and blancmange and jelly. The
moral imperative is thus reinforced: the people of rich countries
are not only adequately fed but are also replete; their refusal to
help the hungry cannot possibly be excused or justified.

David McKee's *Two Monsters* (1985) and *Tusk Tusk* (1978) are
both fables centred on rather similar ideas about the causes of
social conflict; both point to the destructive force of xenophobia
and the human propensity to deep suspicion of and often devas-
tating violence towards those who in trivial ways are unlike us.
In *Tusk Tusk* it is black elephants and white elephants who fight

But recently the little ears and the big ears   have been giving each other strange looks.

Tusk Tusk (McKee, 1978)
Reprinted by permission of Anderson Press from D. McKee (1978) *Tusk Tusk*

each other until they are all killed apart from a few peace-lovers who run away never to be seen again. In *Two Monsters* a red monster and a blue monster live on either side of a mountain and quarrel so violently about whether sunset should be described as day departing or as night arriving that they hurl rocks at each other and eventually destroy the mountain. But in both books there is some hope, even if only qualified optimism is justified by the ending of the stories. The all-grey grandchildren of the vanished pacifist elephants emerge from the jungle to live in peace with each other, except that the last line tells us: 'recently the little ears and the big ears have been giving each other strange looks.'

The two monsters seeing each other for the first time realise that they have much in common. 'Pity about the mountain,' says one of them right at the end, but by then it is too late as the environment has been reduced to a pile of rubble. Although both these picture books are distanced from the real world by the nature of the characters – the monsters are as cuddly as those in *Where the Wild Things Are* (Sendak, 1967) – and by illustrations which are amusingly droll (the elephants use their trunks with amazing versatility) – they still resonate with social and moral significance: for example, black and white elephants may prompt thoughts of racial intolerance and ethnic cleansing, and red and blue monsters may remind us of Protestants and Catholics in Northern Ireland.

The experience of war

Given the diversity of social issues considered in picture books it is not surprising that the supreme conflicts and disasters of war should feature too. If the best-known examples are probably *When the Wind Blows* (Briggs, 1982) and *Maus: A Survivor's Tale* (Spiegelman, 1992), two recent books by Michael Foreman are equally forceful and compelling. In both, much more use is made of the written word than in the picture books considered previously, partly because they are much longer books, partly because they are closer in style and format to that of information texts, and partly because the pictures take different forms and fulfil different functions.

War Boy: A Country Childhood (1989) is an autobiographical account of growing up in an East Anglian coastal town in the years of the Second World War, accompanied by a variety of illustrations such as photographs, copies of cigarette cards and posters of the time, cartoon-style sketches, pen and ink drawings, and full-colour paintings. The text is episodic, characters are described, events narrated, tales told in a discontinuous style, but the family background, the geographical setting and the extraordinary background reality of wartime bind together the stories of growing up, of adults encountered, of childhood adventures. The language is simple without being bland or dull; at times, indeed, the imagery is very striking, as Foreman says of one character: 'her laughter stopped traffic', and of others that: 'a chill would come from their letter-box', and that yet others were 'ominous as vultures'. The tone of the book is often nostalgic, sometimes sentimental, occasionally elegiac; not only is there a pervading sadness for the soldiers and sailors who passed through never to return but there is also an irresistible sense of an ageing man looking back wistfully to a time and a social context which is gone for ever: 'And the memory of those who passed through our village on the way to war will remain

War Boy: A Country Childhood (Foreman, 1989)
Reprinted by permission of Pavilion Books from *War Boy* by Michael Foreman

for ever with the ghosts of us children in the fields and woods of long ago.' Some of the stories Foreman tells are serious, even tragic, like one about a bomb coming through the roof of his house and another about a fire at the church, but there's humour too. The pictures from a collection of cigarette cards about incendiary bombs are accompanied by the wry comment: 'If you collected enough cigarette cards you knew what to do', and there are many funny little anecdotes: the escape of a predatory goat, various ways of annoying old ladies, scrumping for apples in the Vicar's garden, and the one about Sid, 'the man from the Co-op who bought warts. He bought mine for sixpence. He gave me sixpence and my warts disappeared', which exactly captures the magic of childhood and the apparent lunacy of adults. But in addition, from the simplest sketches to the full-colour paintings, the illustrations extend the meanings of the text and provide a forceful stimulus to the imagination of the reader. For example

Mother grabbed me from the bed. The night sky was filled with lights. Searchlights, anti-aircraft fire, stars and a bombers' moon. The sky bounced as my mother ran. Just as we reached our dug-out across the street, the sky flared red as the church exploded.

two paintings early in the book depict, first, Foreman's mother rushing him across the street from their house to the safety of a dug-out with the flames from the exploding church ('The sky bounced') in the background and, second, of the building itself consumed by the fire.

These pictures are not photographic in style, but fluid, flowing and dynamic. The colours of the fire in swathes of red, orange, yellow and pink appear to ebb and flow and the figures running across the road seem almost to move across the page. The outline of the church is barely discernible behind a Celtic cross and the firefighter's efforts are dwarfed by the inferno. These are vivid and expressive pictures, in which one can not only see but also almost feel the heat and the terror of the fire.

The same qualities are apparent in Foreman's dramatic and impassioned sequel, *War Game* (1993), which is dedicated to the memory of his four uncles who all died in the First World War.

After the initial excitement of the four companions from rural Suffolk who join up in 1914 the tone becomes increasingly sombre as the wretched reality of life in the trenches is graphically depicted in both words and pictures. The famous football game between English and German soldiers on Christmas Day provides a lighter interlude but the book ends in death and destruction as Will, one of the four friends, is shown mortally wounded in a shell hole, accompanied only by a dying German soldier:

> At home when he had a bad dream he knew if he opened his eyes, the bad dream would end. But here his eyes were already open.
> Perhaps if he closed them, the nightmare would end.
> He closed his eyes.

In the last three openings the utterly bleak landscape is shown gradually covered with a blanket of snow, and in the last two wordless pictures tiny bright-red poppies begin to appear. This ending is all the more powerful and emotive because of the grounding of the story in the documented history of the time:

He closed his eyes.

War Game (Foreman, 1993)
Reprinted by permission of Pavilion Books from *War Game* by Michael Foreman

the reproductions of recruiting posters and advertisements, the naive enthusiasm of very ordinary and very young men for a great adventure, their obsession with football. The impression left with the reader is not only that the apocalyptic events of the destruction of an entire generation seem horrifying but also that they appear senseless and futile.

Conclusion

There are obviously substantial differences of theme, tone and style in the books briefly considered here but there are also clear connections and continuities between all of them. At the risk of stating the obvious, it may be worth reiterating the elements which in these and many other similar works contribute to what I have described as the moral imperative of picture books.

These are all ideological works; none is or pretends to be indifferent or impartial. Each book is suffused with values and beliefs, each author is passionately opinionated about some aspect of social life as it exists and as it ought to be. The extent to which this is explicit varies: at times, as in *Dinosaurs and All That Rubbish* and *Piggybook*, the author's convictions are substantially overt and upfront, in others like *Who's a Clever Baby Then?* there is a greater degree of subtlety or ambiguity, but in every case the moral commitment of the author can be discerned.

These are all books in which the relationship between words and pictures is central to their effect. In some cases, like *War Boy*, they are mutually reinforcing in a fairly direct way, in others like *Gorilla* and *Not Now Bernard* the relationship is more equivocal, and in yet others, like *Zoo*, the words and the pictures seem at first to be telling quite different stories. Every time, however, it is the way in which the author arranges the relationship, and the way in which the reader responds to it, which creates the reading experience which is characteristic of the genre.

And finally, implicit throughout has been a denial that any of these books can or should be regarded as immature or trivial. They may be used for trivial purposes: *Two Monsters* may be regarded as a handy substitute for a reading scheme text, *Panda's Puzzle* may provide pictures for a geographical topic, *War Game* may be mined for resource material relevant to historical inquiry. It is not that such practices are especially iniquitous,

but that they may negate alternative and much more sophisticated readings.

Notes

1. Serious attention by literary critics to illustrations in novels
for adults is very unusual; a rare exception is a chapter called 'The
Dickens illustrations: their function' in Leavis and Leavis (1970).

2. Coincidentally and almost unbelievably, in the week I
wrote this *Not Now Bernard*, first published nearly twenty years
ago, was the sixteenth best-selling paperback in the UK, according to *The Times*.

3. See also McKee's *I Hate my Teddy Bear* (1982) and *Charlotte's
Piggy Bank* (1996), two more brilliantly allusive works.

4. There is (eventually) an equally happy ending in Annalena
McAfee's *The Visitors who Came to Stay* (1984) for which Browne
provided typically surreal pictures, but a more pessimistic account of family life can be seen in his version of the Brothers
Grimm's *Hansel and Gretel* (1981); but then it is one of the more
lugubrious fairy tales; see Doonan (1983).

5. McKee's own treatment of sexism in *Snow Woman* (1987) is
rather more ambivalent.

6. See also *Willy the Wimp* (1984) and more recently *King Kong*
(1994b).

7. See also Foreman's illustrations in Piers (1984) *Long Neck
and Thunderfoot* and in McCrum (1983) *The Brontosaurus Birthday
Cake*.

Acknowledgements

I am grateful to my colleague Bill Hart for his comments on this
chapter.

Bibliography

Adamson, J. and Adamson, G. (1996) *Topsy and Tim Have Itchy Heads*,
    Harmondsworth: Puffin.
Althea (1982) *When Uncle Bob Died*, London: Dinosaur.
Althea (1987) *I Have Epilepsy*, London: Dinosaur.
Baddeley, P. and Eddershaw, C. (1994) *Not So Simple Picture Books*, Stoke:
    Trentham Books.

Bettelheim, B. and Zelan, K. (1991) *On Learning to Read*, Harmondsworth: Penguin.

Briggs, R. (1982) *When the Wind Blows*, London: Hamish Hamilton.

Brown, M. and Krensky, S. (1983) *Perfect Pigs*, London: Collins.

Browne, A. (1983) *Gorilla*, London: Julia MacRae.

Browne, A. (1984) *Willy the Wimp*, London: Julia MacRae.

Browne, A. (1986) *Piggybook*, London: Julia MacRae.

Browne, A. (1992) *Zoo*, London: Julia MacRae.

Browne, A. (1994a) Making picture books. In Styles, M., Bearne, E. and Watson, V. (eds.) *The Prose and the Passion: Children and their Reading*, London: Cassell.

Browne, A. (1994b) *King Kong*, London: Julia MacRae

De Saint Mars, D. and Bloch, S. (1991) *We're Going to Have a Baby*, London: Fantail.

Dixon, B. (1977) *Catching them Young: Sex, Race and Class in Children's Fiction*, London: Pluto Press.

Doonan, J. (1983) Talking pictures: a new look at *Hansel and Gretel*, *Signal*, 42, pp. 123–31.

Doonan, J. (1993) *Looking at Pictures in Picture Books*, Stroud: Thimble Press.

Foreman, M. (1972) *Dinosaurs and All That Rubbish*, London: Hamish Hamilton.

Foreman, M. (1974) *War and Peas*, London: Hamish Hamilton.

Foreman, M. (1977) *Panda's Puzzle*, London: Hamish Hamilton.

Foreman, M. (1989) *War Boy: A Country Childhood*, London: Pavilion Books.

Foreman, M. (1993) *War Game*, London: Pavilion Books.

Fox, G. (1996) Reading picture books . . . how to? In Styles, M., Bearne, E. and Watson, V. (eds.) *Voices Off: Texts, Contexts and Readers*, London: Cassell.

Gooderham, D. (1993) Still catching them young? The moral dimension in young children's books, *Children's Literature in Education*, 89, pp. 115–22.

Graham, J. (1990) *Pictures on the Page*, Sheffield: National Association for the Teaching of English.

Grimm Bros. (1981) *Hansel and Gretel*, London: Julia MacRae.

Hunt, P. (1994) *An Introduction to Children's Literature*, Oxford: Oxford University Press.

Landsberg, M. (1988) *The World of Children's Books: A Guide to Choosing the Best*, London: Simon & Schuster.

Leavis, F. and Leavis, Q. (1970) *Dicken the Novelist*, London: Chatto & Windus.

Lewis, D. (1990) The constructedness of texts: picture books and the metafictive, *Signal*, 62, pp. 131–46.

Lewis, D. (1996) Getting a grip on the picture book, *Newsletter of Children's Literature Lecturer's Group*, 4, pp. 3–11.

McAfee, A. (1984) *The Visitors who Came to Stay*, London: Hamish Hamilton.

McCrum, R. (1983) *The Brontosaurus Birthday Cake*, London: Hamish Hamilton.

McKee, D. (1978) *Tusk Tusk*, London: Andersen Press.

McKee, D. (1980) *Not Now Bernard*, London: Andersen Press.

McKee, D. (1982) *I Hate my Teddy Bear*, London: Andersen Press.

McKee, D. (1985) *Two Monsters*, London: Andersen Press.

McKee, D. (1987) *Snow Woman*, London: Andersen Press.

McKee, D. (1988) *Who's a Clever Baby Then?* London: Andersen Press.

McKee, D. (1996) *Charlotte's Piggy Bank*, London: Andersen Press.

Meek, M. (1988) *How Texts Teach what Readers Learn*, Stroud: Thimble Press.

Moon, B. (1985) *Practical Ways to Teach Reading*, London: Ward Lock.

Nodelman, P. (1988) *Words about Pictures: The Narrative Art of Children's Picture Books*, Athens, Ga: University of Georgia Press.

Piers, H. (1984) *Long Neck and Thunderfoot*, Harmondsworth: Puffin.
Pithers, D. and Greene, S. (1986) *We Can Say No!* London: Beaver.
Ross, T. (1988) *Super Dooper Jezebel*, London: Andersen Press.
Rushdie, S. (1995) *The Moor's Last Sigh*, London: Jonathan Cape.
Sendak, M. (1967) *Where the Wild Things Are*, London: Bodley Head.
Spiegelman, A. (1992) *Maus: A Survivor's Tale*, London: Deutsch.
Stephens, J. (1992) *Language and Ideology in Children's Fiction*, London: Longman.
Stones, R. (1983) *'Pour out the Cocoa, Janet': Sexism in Children's Books*, London: Longman for Schools Council.
Stones, R. (1991) *Children Don't Divorce*, London: Dinosaur.
Storrie, J. (1989) *Living with Mum*, London: Dinosaur.

Chapter 2

Turning the visual into the verbal: children reading wordless books

Judith Graham

The publication of *Clown* by Quentin Blake in 1995 and its winning of the Ragazzi Prize in Bologna in 1996 has stirred me to reconsider the phenomenon of the wordless picture book for children and to inspect the 'reading' of some of these books, including *Clown*, by children aged between 5 and 12. I am interested in both the special artifact that is the wordless book and also in the ways in which child readers turn one medium into another when we ask them to tell the story of the pictures in a wordless book.

Clown is Quentin Blake's first and, to date, only wordless book, though many of his early books such as *Patrick* (1968) and *Jack and Nancy* (1969) (conceived as films) can be understood without the lines of written text. Is it surprising that an illustrator as visually fluent as Quentin Blake has produced only one wordless book in over forty years of illustrating? One has to answer no. There are in fact very few wordless books compared with the number of picture books on the market. Amongst illustrators in the UK, I can only think of Peter Collington for whom the wordless book is the preferred medium. Several illustrators, including Charles Keeping, Brian Wildsmith, Pat Hutchins, Shirley Hughes, Raymond Briggs, Jan Ormerod, Philippe Dupasquier and John Prater, have produced perhaps one or two titles but many more illustrators, including the most eminent and established, have never attempted the form. Whilst there has been a steady trickle of wordless books throughout the last thirty years, both in the UK, the USA and on the continent, there has never been the flood that some predicted (and some feared) and nor has the form been declared of major importance, neither to the history of children's literature nor to the development of children's literacy.

It is perhaps not too difficult to account for the low profile of wordless books. They are generally not respected by parents who, however mistakenly, regard them as contributing little to their young children's literacy or literary growth. Teachers, mindful of parental opposition, may also feel cautious of this form and preserve their budgets for books with words though they may note, in passing, their pupils' enthusiasm for Raymond Briggs' *The Snowman* (1978). Publishers have to take note of these widespread reservations and may not wish to have too many wordless books on their lists. Illustrators themselves, however much they are attracted to the challenge of telling a story through pictures alone, know that nothing is more time-consuming than the scores of individual pictures that are necessary to create a full-length story. In addition, many may derive more inspiration from the initial stimulus of an author's written text or may enjoy the balancing of the two media if they are composing written text as well. So the wordless book is not the most popular form and one wonders why it is attempted at all.

One explanation must be that it gives an illustrator great satisfaction to achieve the telling of a story without the use of words. To use visual means only – line, colour, space, framing, angles, close-ups and long-shots and everything else in between – to capture the narrative flow of a story, to give form to ideas, to record visually the observations one makes in life about people is a great achievement.

Another explanation may be that the illustrator in a wordless book has a guarantee that his or her pictures will be looked at. We know that children (unlike many adults) do look at all pictures with care but we also know that written text dictates to some extent what we 'see' in the picture and that we may ignore those details to which we are not directed. Thus, in *Where the Wild Things Are* (Sendak, 1963), when Max is sent to bed without

The Great Escape (Dupasquier, 1988)
© P. Dupasquier (1988). Reprinted by permission of the publisher, Walker Books Ltd., London

any supper, we look for his reaction because the words have alerted us. We notice less the details in his room – the fact that his window has shutters for instance – unless we are children looking whilst an adult reads. The absence of words in wordless books may mean that pictures are scanned more thoroughly. Do illustrators enjoy this prospect? I imagine so.

A further explanation may be the belief held that the wordless picture book is a generous invitation to the child reader to create the verbal story at will and that, because of this 'openness', the book will retain the attraction for the child that comes from co-creation. Thus one 'reader' may tell the opening page of *The Great Escape* (Dupasquier, 1988) in these words: 'The prisoner was going to be run over by the motor bike so he swerved and ran behind the delivery van and then he saw a shop with red and white blinds so he ran in there.' Another may say: 'The man gets out of the gates while they are open 'cos they're delivering some food and the guards in the watchtowers see him so they come rushing down and they all see him going into a shop.' Both readers have made the text 'tell' in ways satisfying to themselves. There are potentially many more ways of 'telling the page', in any number of sentences and with a limitless choice of words. The child chooses the path through and the theory is that the book is more significant because of this 'ownership' and the bonding with the book that occurs. Illustrators may enjoy offering this co-creating opportunity to children.

A final explanation may be that talented illustrators think in visual terms and see no reason to use words – their own or others' – if they can achieve their effects without. It is possible that the need to 'trim' illustrations to written text is a frustration to some illustrators and that the effect of being able to include just exactly what you want to, with no consideration having to be given to the written text, is very liberating.

Whilst some or all of the above may account for an illustrator's attraction to the form, an illustrator who decides to create a book for children without words accepts that there will be losses as well as gains. Pictures can do many things and they can do some things that words are less good at but they cannot do everything that words can do. Pictures show us what characters look like, what they are wearing, how they hold themselves, what they are doing and what they are looking at; they can show us settings and create mood and atmosphere. They show most successfully a sequence of events and are able to record several things happening in the same scene. They can, with a focus on gesture and facial expression, indicate what characters are feeling and, in so far as facial expression and body 'language' reveal thought, they can hint at what is passing through characters' minds.

Illustrations cannot, however, tell us what things and people are called nor the words that people are actually saying or thinking. Illustrations, whilst they can very successfully tell us a story in a linear fashion, cannot tell us what has happened in the past nor what is planned to happen later, except by resorting to speech/thought 'bubbles', a graphic convention that Quentin Blake uses in *Clown*. Nor, rather obviously, can a wordless picture book indulge in word play nor develop a counterpointed rhythm with a line or more of written text.

One has only to look at the recently published *Handa's Surprise* (Browne, 1994) to realise that the story of Handa's 'surprise present' would be a different thing had the tale been told, as to some extent it could have been, without words. We would lose Handa's interior monologue as she names and describes the fruits in the basket on her head: 'sweet-smelling guava', 'tangy purple passion-fruit.' We would lose the irony in the word 'surprise' which, when used by Handa at the beginning is a surprise for her friend; by the end, the surprise becomes Handa's when she sees her exotic fruits are replaced by tangerines. We would never know, from pictures alone, that tangerines were her friend's favourite fruit. Over and above this, we would lose the characteristic electric charge found in many picture books, where the written text does *not* alert us to what is happening in the pictures. Thus, in *Handa's Surprise* the tension that mounts as Handa's fruits are systematically plundered by various animals is all the more real as the narrator, who should be looking and warning the oblivious Handa, is blithely chattering on about creamy green avocados and spiky-leaved pineapples.

The different ways in which words and pictures work, each ignoring the other's message, mean that the deliberate contradictions between the two enable an irony to emerge in much the same way as in the well-known *Rosie's Walk* (Hutchins, 1968). This is one of the elements of the picture book that wordless books have to sacrifice.

Will she like the soft yellow banana ...

Handa's Surprise (Browne, 1994)
© E. Brown (1994). Reprinted by permission of the publisher, Walker
Books Ltd, London

In the reading or 'beholding' of a wordless picture book, the
reader becomes the narrator, with all that that implies for co-
creating and bonding to the book as I have discussed above. But
it is a rare child reader who can narrate a text with the shaping,
the description, the dialogue and particularly the irony that
emerges from *Handa's Surprise*. Indeed, few adults could produce such a text, even after time to familiarise themselves with
the book and time to devise a running line of written text. Nor
should we expect such a thing but long familiarity on both
adults' and children's parts with picture books tends to ac-
custom us to these extra pleasures which wordless books have
to forgo. It seemed to me that the children, with whom I was
working and to whom I am now going to turn, revealed not just
a longing for the written word and the frisson it creates but also
the fluency that their reading (or remembering) of a rich verbal
text gave them. In *Les mots* (1964), the infant Jean Paul Sartre is

amazed at the verbal fluency of his mother which emerges when she reads compared to her hesitancy when she tells made-up stories and he longs to possess that fluency himself. For the children I worked with it was no different. There is no doubt that their tellings were of a different order from those elicited by the rewarding written texts that they were used to (even if their readings of these books were 'remembered readings') and I think that on one level they disappointed themselves that they did not sound more impressive (though they were very interesting to me). Anne Rowe (1996, p. 232), in her important chapter 'Voices off' in the book of the same name, talks of the reader of wordless books being placed 'in the position of being universal narrator without the authority of knowing the future or of necessarily knowing what is significant'. Particularly for the child reader, the responsibility of turning the visual into the verbal may sometimes be more than they wish for.

The quiet longing for a picture book with words that some of the 5 and 6-year-olds with whom I had worked is understandable for another reason. I was the one choosing the wordless books for my own purposes and they longed to show off their emerging reading skills with books such as the Ahlbergs' *Each Peach Pear Plum* (1978) or David McKee's *Not Now Bernard* (1980) which they could see in my bag. They found, especially initially, the reading of wordless books much harder work than any other reading they had ever done. Far from being 'too easy', a comment frequently heard in relation to wordless books, they were very challenging. There are several reasons for this finding. The creator of a wordless book eschews words. The words, as described above, direct the reader's eye to what is significant in the picture or, with deliberate disdain, encourage us to notice what they have neglected. Both these activities require less effort than the scanning of every picture to discover the significant. Perry Nodelman (1988, p. 187) is in no doubt that the reading of books without words requires training and that several interconnected skills are necessary 'if we are to find stories in a sequence of pictures'. The young children I worked with were *very* tired when they had finished reading a Collington or a Dupasquier title or the Quentin Blake text. They were doubly tired if their experience of narrative was as yet so limited that the task as they construed it was to tell what they saw on every page, rather than to link pictures because they could detect the narrative thread running through them.

In truth, illustrators know that, in dispensing with words, they are by no means creating an easy book or a book for children who cannot read. Whilst there are a few wordless books that particularly appeal to and are 'read' by preliterate children – and Jan Ormerod's *Sunshine* (1981) is pre-eminently in this category – on the whole, wordless books demand sophisticated narrative skills. Whilst wordless books can teach these narrative skills to some extent, you need to have a sense of what is logical and possible in a story. A 4-year-old, reading *Sunshine* for the first time, construed the spreading blackness from the burning toast as night falling. The whole book only covers a family's getting-up period before going off to work and school so to bring about a premature dusk was certainly to disrupt the rhythm of the book. A second reading saw the same child connecting elements of the pictures and reading the signs more rationally. Such examples of 'misreadings' had been noticed with other children on previous occasions (Graham, 1987; 1990). Perry Nodelman (1988, p. 190) records the difficulties that his

The Story of a Little Mouse Trapped in a Book (Felix, 1980)
Reprinted from M. Felix *The Story of a Little Mouse Tapped in a Book* by permission of Moonlight Publishing Ltd.

5-year-old son has with imputing motivation to the character's actions in a wordless book, concluding that the 'lack of sophist-ication of his visual story-making competence' lay behind the difficulty.

The youngest child (Andrew) with whom I worked was also 5 years old and he had never seen a wordless book before. Here is his response to the very first book I showed him: *The Story of a Little Mouse Trapped in a Book* (Felix, 1980):

> Andrew: This doesn't have any writing so how can I tell the story? A mouse pushed, a mouse running away, going 'ooh'. This is a white page. How do I tell about this? Then I saw it biting a hole, biting a big square. How did he get out? I don't know. He's going to make a paper aeroplane to go down. Now he's down on the ground.

I then showed him Monique Felix's second 'mouse' book: *Another Story of the Little Mouse Trapped in a Book* (1983), hoping that some of the uncertainty would have disappeared:

> Andrew: It's just the same as the other one (*slams book shut. Re-opens it*).
> He bites his finger. He's thinking – shall I make a paper aero-plane? No, a paper boat 'cos of the sea. He's going backwards.

The perplexed response to the wordless page is not voiced when he meets the second book (and nor was it ever voiced again). Is Andrew a particularly fast learner or is only one exposure to the form enough for all children? In addition, Andrew dispenses with his own role as viewer ('Then I saw it biting a hole') and he asks no more rhetorical questions. The verbalising of the little mouse's thoughts is a very promising response but the narrative shape of the book still escapes him and he does not read the final picture (which is a rear view of the mouse) as the conventional 'sailing away into the sunset' image.

Here he is now with the third book of Monique Felix, *The Colors* (1991):

> Andrew (*explores the cover*): The mouse has nibbled the cover. It's not really the mouse – it's the man who made the book. Is it the same again or a bit different? He sees . . . he's in a book. Oh! I get it. That's a table and a person is running through the door. That's red glue or toothpaste. Ah, it's paint. He draws a picture. Now he's gone to get another colour. Then he gets two to mix. He's stepping on it and it'll make orange (*remaining pages turned without comment*).

Another Story of the Little Mouse Trapped in a Book (Felix, 1983)
Reprinted from M. Felix *Another Story of the Little Mouse Trapped in a Book* by permission of Moonlight Publishing Ltd

Here I think we see more involvement and enthusiasm, an interesting reflection on the physical aspect of the book, a promising prediction and the start of a narrative shape. The 'Oh! I get it' suggests that he sees the task as problem-solving which, in fact, the reading of a wordless book often resembles. His silent reading of the last few pages of the book seemed to me to be a wish to find out what happened without having to verbalise everything – or indeed anything. The benefit of this exposure to wordless books for Andrew would be very hard to assess at this point but reading-like strategies that are relevant to the reading of all texts are emerging and, if confirmed, they might well be usefully consolidated.

These readings by Andrew were markedly different from those given by two girls: Harriet who is very nearly 6 and Clelia who is just over 6 and fully bilingual. They both interpreted my request to share these books with me as an invitation to give a running commentary on what they saw in the pictures:

Harriet: He's looking up. He's peeping. He's running. He's eating the wall. He's looking out, down at all the animals. Now he's opening and making a square. He sees some clouds. He sees the house again. He sees the clouds again. Now he's folding some paper and making an aeroplane and he's flying and that is the end.

> Clelia: He is pulling . . . running . . . sniffing . . . eating . . . look-
> ing . . . seeing . . . opening . . . closing . . . bending it . . . folding it
> . . . making a plane . . . going in it. He eats.

Harriet makes an effort to record not only the mouse's efforts to escape from the book but also to record what the mouse sees – the countryside scene that he glimpses beyond the book to which he ultimately descends. Clelia focuses entirely on the actions of the little mouse, which is obviously the first narrative challenge; she would appear to believe that the mouse needs to be reported on objectively. The countryside scene needs no description from her any more than, if she were reporting on the Grand National, she would feel the need to tell her listeners what the horses can see. When asked to reread in her second language, Clelia produced an exact translation of her first reading, neither adding nor subtracting anything.

At this point, I needed to pause for reflection. I tried to account for what I felt were the limited responses to the books. Monique Felix's books are probably more appealing to adults than to children and the cleverness of the exploitation of the book form – the meta-fictive game-playing going on – was not obviously appreciated by the children on these first readings. But I was more disappointed in the restricted language that was emerging. Clelia's language use was so economical that it verged on the monotonous and yet I knew that she was a most competent language user in both her languages and that, in addition, she was very familiar with books. Harriet likewise was an extraordinarily fluent speaker and loved stories. (Neither girl was reading conventional texts independently yet.) The children were all willing to share these books with me but were not really enthusiastic. I was not convinced that they were 'discovering their voices' and 'enjoying a rewarding sense of co-creation' from this encounter with wordless books.

I had noticed that all children, when invited to 'read this book for me', 'told' the books in the present tense which is not surprising as they have been put into the position of commentator on events whose outcome they do not know. If you report on a Cup Final or on the Grand Prix you similarly use the present tense. Indeed, in all the tellings of wordless books I collected, even from adults, the present tense was always used. I decided to be more interventionist. I invited Harriet to read the second 'little mouse' book but I suggested that she might like to start with the story opening, 'Once upon a time'. She took up this idea enthusiastically:

> Harriet: Once upon a time a mouse was running away from a cat. He stopped and nibbled the page of the book and then he thought for a minute. He was pecking at the page. He was trapped in a book. He saw loads of seagulls and some dippy divers and skate boards and lifeboat and a rowing boat and the lifeboat was going off. He made a little paper boat for himself to go rowing – out of the page – and he just sailed away over the deep blue sea.

I was impressed by this reading and I think that Harriet herself suddenly felt that her story-telling fluency was returning. She has no problem sustaining the narrative past tense, she includes ample detail and her ending is most eloquent. I was very keen to find Andrew and Clelia again to offer them the same opportunity to retell with the traditional 'Once upon a time' opening. When I did see Clelia again, two weeks had elapsed and she had a much younger child, David, with her. I suggested that she might like to tell the story to David before she showed him the pictures, and that she should tell it as a story. As with Harriet, the prospect was instantly attractive to her. I offered her both the 'little mouse' books, the second of which she had not seen before. She chose the familiar one first but also wanted to 'do' the other one. Here is her first reading:

> Clelia: Once upon a time there was a little mouse. He was stuck in a book. (*Aside, in a dropped voice: we can see him looking up.*) He pushed and he pushed and he pushed but he didn't manage. He couldn't get out. He was getting really thirsty and crying too. Then he nibbled and he nibbled (*aside, in a dropped voice: he was nibbling the page*) and he nibbled and he nibbled. Then he opened the page and he saw a farmer's house and a tractor. Then he cut nearly all the page (*aside, in a dropped voice: we can see a bit of the cornfield*) and then he pulled the page (*aside: there's clouds and hens and such*). Then he folded the page again and again and again and then rain was pouring down. Everyone had to take in their washing and go into the house. Finally he made the plane and a rainbow came out. Birds were singing, some ducks were going in the puddles made by the rain and a little cat was in the fields too. Then he went in his aeroplane and flew off and nibbled some corn in the cornfield. The End.

This was an utterly different retelling from the first telling recorded above. Amongst other achievements, one notes her dramatic use of repetition, her handling of the dual-narrative and her willingness to include the detail of the scenery. Her command over the past tense never wavered and her asides (her own idea) were not distracting. David then asked to see the pictures. Clelia took him through the book, saying 'and here's where I said such and such' (with total recall of her actual words though she added, 'the little mouse is a bit astonished'). Her listener looked only at the pictures of the mouse, not at the scenes beyond the mouse which is probably what Clelia herself did on first reading and his only comment was 'ah! he's making an aeroplane!' Clelia wanted to hold forth to David with the second book, as yet unseen by her. I was interested to see if she would be able to put together an equally coherent telling:

> Clelia: Once upon a time, there was a scared little mouse and he was so tired that he fell down. He touched his forehead – he was boiling hot. He nibbled and he rested a bit and thought. He nibbled again. He was stuck. Then he put out his hand and got out. Under the page. Then he folded it. The sea was splashing him so he hid under the page. He made a little boat and sailed away on the sea, looking at the sky. And he lived happily ever after.

Whilst from Clelia I have no first retelling with which to compare, I predict that without my invitation to tell in the narrative past tense, using the 'Once upon a time' opening, the telling would have been as limited as her telling of the first 'little mouse' book. In addition, the presence of her audience, needing a full account because he could not see the pictures, was pushing Clelia to be more explicit. The reading is not as competent as on the familiar text but that should not surprise us. She has more difficulty in integrating into the narrative the details from the 'outside scene' but the attempt at interpreting the mouse's gestures is impressive and it is this detecting of motivation that gives the narrative a coherence, remarkable for a first reading.

Andrew, when I invited a retelling with a 'Once upon a time' opening, also found a more fluent voice and increased commitment. Where before we had, 'He's going to make a paper aeroplane to go down. Now he's down on the ground' now we had, 'the mouse had a whole page now and he folded it in half. He looked down at the village and it started raining in the village. There was a rainbow and he went in the aeroplane and he nibbled some wheat on the ground.'

I was now in no doubt that the wordless book was full of potential for those aspects claimed for it, provided that the reader was encouraged to tell in the past tense. I was very keen to try my readers out on *Clown* but felt that I had to work up to this, especially with these younger children. We read Philippe Dupasquier's *I Can't Sleep* (1990) and *The Great Escape* (1988), Fernando Krahn's *How Santa Claus had a Long and Difficult Journey Delivering his Presents* (1971) (the long title of this book almost disqualifies it as a wordless book) and Peter Collington's *The Angel and the Soldier Boy* (1987). None of the children independently began in the past tense but in every instance, fluency and a sense of mastery improved when the child was started off with the traditional past-tense story opening. In addition, some textual difficulties – such as the house layout in *I Can't Sleep* where it needs to be appreciated that the parents' and the children's bedrooms are on different floors – seemed to melt away when telling in the past tense rather than in the present. Implications are more fully explored in language that is right at the edge

From: *Clown*, by Quentin Blake, © 1995 by Quentin Blake. Reprinted by permission of Henry Holt & Company, Inc., and by permission of Jonathan Cape, London.

of these children's competence. In *The Angel and the Soldier Boy*, Harriet's initial line 'she picks up the sword and she's crying' becomes 'she bent down and picked up the sword. She recognised it and started to cry.'

I finish with *Clown* and we return to Harriet and a reading that was not influenced by any suggestions on my part:

Harriet (*looking at cover*): This looks exciting. The city's very big; the clown is very funny.

(*Looking at title page.*) Oh! it's a toy. I always think my toys come alive when my mum and dad go out. They play when I'm out as well. I'm looking at it and thinking about it. Reminds me of *Toy Story* – in someone's imagination but you have to be a toy.

(*Turns page.*) She wants to throw all the toys in the dustbin – they're old.

(*Turns page.*) What I think is – the clown is coming alive and it's getting out. He's lost his foot – or his shoes are under all the rest.

(*Turns page.*) He's found a trainer and he's putting it on. He's running. The baby can see the clown. She'll run off to get him. I ran off in the supermarket. That mummy – is it a mummy? – might have the clown for the baby.

(*Turns page.*) The clown's telling the baby that . . . that the mummy . . . on the other page (*turns back*) the mummy who threw the toys away . . . it's in the bubble . . .

(*Turns page.*) The baby can't do anything because the mummy's pulled her. The clown's saying, 'Oh no! Now I can't do anything about my friends'. A man picks him up and puts him in a contest – a dressing-up contest. I was in a contest and I was angry 'cos I didn't win. My mum put pipe cleaners in my hair 'cos I was Wendy. I think the clown will win 'cos he's the smallest.

(*Turns page.*) There's the bubble mark again – and he's telling the girl but the chance is lost again 'cos there's another person coming – a grandma.

(*Turns page.*) She's tooken her home to her mum. Her mum has thrown the clown out of the window 'cos she's already got one. 'This yucky clown is not coming to our home.' She's very rich – she' s got a big room. The little girl is still in fancy dress.

(*Turns page.*) It's tumbling through the trees and then splat! He's still thinking about his friends – 'cos the dustbin men might come.

(*Turns page.*) The dog's trying to copy him. Then a big man comes – he might be a giant 'cos it doesn't tell you all of it.

(*Turns page.*) A really big man tosses it away – it looks like it's flying.

(*Turns page.*) Now it's come into a bedroom and the baby's crying. It's doing a somersault and the baby's much more happy – they want to keep it.

From: *Clown*, by Quentin Blake, © 1995 by Quentin Blake. Reprinted by permission of Henry Holt & Company, Inc., and by permission of Jonathan Cape, London.

(*Turns page – long pause.*) Now the clown's telling the girl what's happened and there's another wicked girl in the bubble. The clown's helping the girl and doing the bed.

(*Turns page.*) He's changing the nappy and they're getting ready to go out.

(*Turns page.*) And they got back to the toys

(*Turns page.*) and they came home

(*Turns page.*) much more happier.

(*Turns page.*) The end.

Some characteristic features of the first reading of a wordless book emerge from this transcript. First, Harriet relates what is happening to her own first-hand experiences (her toys also come alive, she ran off in a supermarket once, she was in a fancy-dress competition once). We should note that these comments are confined to the beginning of her telling. Secondly, she makes some predictions: the baby will run off to get the clown, the clown will win the fancy-dress competition. Thirdly, she has some queries: 'is it a mummy?' Finally, of course, she tells her story in the present tense except for the last few lines when possibly echoes of the familiar past tense of narrative text reassert themselves.

In addition, atypically in my experience from less confident children, Harriet provides some dialogue for the characters: 'Oh no! Now I can't do anything about my friends.' 'This yucky clown is not coming to our home.' And she attributes motive to the characters' behaviour: toys are thrown out because they are old, the rich lady throws out the clown because they've already got one and, also, because it's 'yucky', the clown's anxiety about his friends is because the dustbin men might come. Harriet also reveals a developed knowledge of the visual conventions employed by Quentin Blake, such as thought bubbles and the partial images as well as following the intended order of the images, which are to be read from top to bottom, left to right as with conventional written text. Finally, we should note how Harriet is well able to decide the social status (of, for instance, the 'rich' lady in her big room) from her careful attention to the detail that Quentin Blake provides in his pictures.

In many ways, then, Harriet's first reading of *Clown* is impressive for a child not yet 6. I asked two older children, Lucy aged 9 and Alex aged 12, to share *Clown* with me and, though there were several interesting differences, in essence the readings were very similar. Neither Lucy nor Alex had experienced wordless books in their recent past and the older child asked to scan the book first but in effect got the measure of the book in a few pages and then launched into his retelling. The major differences between these older children and Harriet were as follows:

- *More elaborate vocabulary* Lucy: The clown 'clambers' out of the dustbin; the clown 'tells about the situation' in the dustbin. Alex: The clown 'delves' in the bin; the mother throws clown away 'in disgust'.
- *More explanation* Lucy: The dog is 'stunned by the clown's acrobats'; the mother is 'not in the house otherwise she'd be helping the baby'. Alex: The tree 'breaks the clown's fall'; the clown 'performs some desperate acrobatics' which 'bewilder' the dog; mother comes home 'stressed'.
- *More indirect speech* Lucy: 'The girl says that her mother will be very happy when she comes back.' Alex: 'She says that her mum will be pleased.'

- *More generalising* Lucy: Woman is 'spring-cleaning'; 'when the mother sees the state of the house, she is delighted.' Alex: 'He keeps thinking about his friends in the dustbin.'
- *More appreciation of irony (from the 12-year-old only)* Alex. 'The dog is not quite so brave after all, in spite of his studded collar.'
- *More use of colloquialisms (from the 12-year-old only)* Alex: The clown 'thinks he looks cool in his trainers'.
- *More understanding of the layers of meaning in the book (from the 12-year-old only)* Alex: 'The girl and the clown look at each other and keep the secret to themselves.'

As I had now come to expect, when the instruction is 'Tell me the story that the pictures tell', the response was once again to tell in the present tense. What I did not expect was that both older children, on being asked to retell using the opening 'Once upon a time', did not sustain their narratives in the past tense beyond the first two sentences. Within seconds, they were back into the present tense again and thus, perhaps, performing with less flair than they might otherwise have managed. My working explanations were that as they were both fluent readers they saw the task as utterly different from reading a written story and that the requirement to shape in any truly literate way was not of interest to them.

The use of the present tense is widespread in children's retelling of wordless books. Unless they have been encouraged to take on the traditional all-seeing, all-knowing narrator's role, by someone suggesting that they begin with 'Once upon a time', it seems that to record the events as they unfold as in a running commentary is the normal response. This is understandable as the present tense tends not to close down the book – the child can keep adding more verbal descriptions of what he or she sees without having to reformulate the words already spoken. However, in the limited work that I record here, there is evidence that the wordless book can be less than enjoyable to those children who, used to reading-like behaviour with picture books, miss the fluency that memory of the written text gives. They certainly miss the characteristic interplay that is possible between words and pictures in the picture book. However, with the encouragement to form a narrative using the past tense, the move from the visual to the verbal is much more assured, at least in the child who is not yet a fluent reader, and the evidence is persuasive that the experience then becomes enjoyable and beneficial. The wordless book for children may well remain a relative rarity for reasons explored in the earlier part of this chapter but the skill and sheer labour of those illustrators who do turn to the form should not go unrecognised. If we give their intended readers the optimum conditions in which to study the books and in which to fashion a verbal telling, wordless books can confirm children as competent interpreters and as fluent and creative language users.

Bibliography

Ahlberg, A. and Ahlberg, J. (1978) *Each Peach Pear Plum*, London: Viking Kestrel.

Blake, Q. (1968) *Patrick*, London: Jonathan Cape.

Blake, Q. (1969) *Jack and Nancy*, London: Jonathan Cape.

Blake, Q. (1995) *Clown*, London: Jonathan Cape.

Briggs, R. (1978) *The Snowman*, London: Hamish Hamilton.

Browne, E. (1994) *Handa's Surprise*, London: Walker Books.

Collington, P. (1987) *The Angel and the Soldier Boy*, London: Methuen Children's Books.

Dupasquier, P. (1988) *The Great Escape*, London: Walker Books.

Dupasquier, P. (1990) *I Can't Sleep*, London: Walker Books.

Felix, M. (1980) *The Story of a Little Mouse Trapped in a Book*, London: Methuen/Moonlight.

Felix, M. (1983) *Another Story of the Little Mouse Trapped in a Book*, London: Methuen/Moonlight.

Felix, M. (1991) *The Colors*, New York: Stewart, Tabori & Chang.

Graham, J. (1987) Texts that teach: wordless picture books, *Language Matters*, no. 1, pp. 22–4.

Graham, J. (1990) *Pictures on the Page*, Sheffield: NATE.

Hutchins, P. (1968) *Rosie's Walk*, London: Bodley Head.

Krahn, F. (1971) *How Santa Claus had a Long and Difficult Journey Delivering his Presents*, London: Longman Young Books.

McKee, D. (1980) *Not Now Bernard*, London: Andersen Press.

Nodelman, P. (1988) *Words about Pictures*, Athens, Ga: University of Georgia Press.

Ormerod, J. (1981) *Sunshine*, London: Penguin/Viking.

Rowe, A. (1996) Voices off – reading wordless picture books. In *Voices Off*, ed. Styles, M., Bearne, E. and Watson, V., London: Cassell.

Sartre, J.P. (1964) *Les mots*, Paris: Gallimard.

Sendak, M. (1963) *Where the Wild Things Are*, New York: Bodley Head.

Chapter 3

Nursery children using illustrations in shared readings and rereadings

Brenda Parkes

This chapter explores how emergent readers utilise the illustrations in picture story books in their quest for meaning and draws upon examples of work from a three-year ethnographic study which documented, described and analysed the experiences of two preschool children with their favourite picture story books. Over time, the two children increasingly involved themselves in transactions with the authors and illustrators of these books and with experienced readers to go well beyond the surface features of the text. In doing so, they developed a range of strategies for meaning-making which were consistent with a transactional approach to reading. While the study reported on the children's transactions with both print and illustrations, this discussion will focus on how one child, Sarah, made use of illustrations to derive meaning from the text.

The benefits of reading aloud to children have been well documented over a long period in literature reporting on emergent literacy (Huey, 1908; Durkin, 1966; Wells, 1982; Baghban, 1984). Researchers, educators and parents generally agree that the practice provides a sound basis for learning to read (Holdaway, 1979; Cochran-Smith, 1984; Dombey, 1989).

More recently, the act of rereading favourite books has been researched in both home and school settings (Martinez and

Roser, 1985; Yaden, 1988; Sulzby, 1987; Parkes, 1990). One of the major findings of this research was that repeated readings of the same text by the same participants never came out the same way. Each time children returned to a text, either independently or with an experienced reader, they did something different. This included asking an experienced reader to read, and just listening; focusing on some aspect of language or illustration; using the illustrations to retell the story in oral language, story language or a mixture of these; and opting to read the story to a reader and using that reader to 'fill in the gaps' when they could not continue independently. As children became more familiar with the books and as their experiential and linguistic facility increased, so too did their interactions. They noticed similarities within and across books; made text to life and life to text connections; and borrowed some of the language of the books to use for their own purposes. In short, the books became a lived-in and lived-through experience. A further finding was recognition of the active role children assumed as meaning-makers.

A semiotic perspective

Research which views language processes through semiotic theory (Harste *et al.*, 1984; Parkes, 1990) has provided new perspectives for examining how children learn. Harste *et al.* (1984, p. 208) state that a semiotic view is one in which 'the orchestration of all signifying structures from all available communication systems in the event have an integral part to play'. A semiotic perspective suggests that communication is an open system. In other words, each time a learner returns to a text, the interpretation will be unique because of the transaction between what the learner currently knows and understands, and how the learner perceives and interprets the available clues in language and illustrations. Each of these interactions could be described as 'a perpetual firstness'. When viewed this way, picture story books become meaning potentials and meaning is created through interactions involving the reader's prior knowledge and experience with the book, the reader's purpose for returning to the book and the sign complex formed by print and illustrations.

Illustrations as sign potentials

Illustrators play a vital role in creating sign potentials in picture story books. It is the illustrator who provides the visual context in which the language is set, and who decides what signs will be embedded in the illustrations to assist the reader in meaning-making. The illustrations complement and extend the written language, bringing characters, settings and events to life. Frequently, the illustrator enters into a special intimacy with young

When Joseph was a baby, his grandfather made him a wonderful blanket . . .

Something from Nothing (Gilman, 1992)
Something from Nothing text and illustrations copyright © 1992 by Phoebe Gilman. Reprinted by permission of Scholastic Canada Ltd, 123 Newkirk Road, Richmond Hill, ON L4C 3GF

readers, inviting them to become insiders as they discover and share artfully concealed details which form a subtext, or an extra dimension to some features of the story. Examples of this include Phoebe Gilman's book, *Something from Nothing* (1992), where she illustrates a family of mice under the floorboards of grandpa's house. Each picture is filled with detail as the industrious mice utilise the fabric scraps which drop through the cracks as grandpa refashions Joseph's blanket again and again. The detail engages the reader in an extra layer of dialogue with the illustrator as they search this illustrated subtext to find how the mice are utilising the scraps.

In *Come away from the Water, Shirley*, John Burningham (1977) juxtaposes each double-page spread with contrasting illustrations. On the one side Shirley's sedate parents are shown in dull colours, reading the newspaper and admonishing her against the perils of enjoying herself. The other side uses bright colours to show Shirley's riotous imaginary adventures with a pirate crew who happen to have anchored nearby. Like the fox in Pat Hutchin's *Rosie's Walk* (1969), Shirley's adventures with the pirates are never mentioned in the written text. That part of the story is created in the children's minds purely through the illustrations. Children delight in finding such details that not only take them well beyond the surface structure of the books but also include them as contributing co-authors and co-illustrators.

In the modern classic *Rosie's Walk*, no mention is made in the written text of the fox who is stalking the seemingly unaware Rosie. This part of the story is completely and perfectly told through a repetitive pattern of intent and mishap which befalls the fox.

Illustrations as meaning potentials

Together with the written language, the illustrations form potential messages on texts. In any given instance, only some aspects of the meaning potential are selected for signification and these are determined by the learner's purpose, his or her personal history of experience and the context of use. Over time, learners generate a multiplicity of interpretations within each book.

Mind you don't get any of that filthy tar
on your nice new shoes

Come away from the Water, Shirley (Burningham, 1977)
From J. Burningham (1977) *Come Away from the Water, Shirley*.
Reprinted by permission of Jonathan Cape

This is clearly illustrated in the example of 2-year-old Sarah
returning to Eric Carle's book *The Very Hungry Caterpillar* (1969)
to fulfil personal agendas. Here Sarah is 'reading' the book to
her mother, and has chosen to begin with the double-page
spread on food. Capercake is a cupcake, but is firmly established
as a capercake (caterpillar cake), her favourite, and a treat she
sometimes receives when they go shopping. The picture acts as
a sign potential for a discussion about how she enjoys her 'ca-
percakes' and she then reads her version of the remainder of the
text:

Mother: What are you doing?
Sarah: Reading.
Mother: Oh!
Sarah: I'm going to see. I'm going capercake, that capercake hey.
Mother: That's a capercake?
Sarah: Yeh.
Mother: Mmm.
Sarah: I like it capercake.
Mother: Pardon?
Sarah: I like it capercake.
Mother: Yeh, Sarah had a capercake.
Sarah: Yeh.

Mother: Was it nice?
Sarah: I get me's got capercake nice.
Mother: Mmm.

Sarah is also very interested in colours in her world at this time and she instigates this discussion about the title page of the book which has a rectangle of coloured dots. She thinks the coloured dots are a 'Smarties' packet, a favourite sweet which she calls 'num nums'. Colour, size and shape and the food theme of the book created the sign potentials for this hypothesis:

Sarah: Nice num nums (*points to coloured dots on the end papers*).
Mother: Yeh, nice num nums. Lots of colours.
Sarah: Yeh, where colour at?
Mother: Yellow.
Sarah: Where's colour at . . . yellow?
Mother: Yeh.
Sarah: Where's colour at this one?
Mother: Orange.
Sarah: What's this one at?
Mother: Pink. The very hungry . . .
Sarah: What's this one say? What's this pink?
Mother: Blue.
Sarah: Blue, what's this one?

Mother: That's brown. Look at this. That says to Sarah, with love
from Da and Poppa.
Sarah: What's this one?

It seems evident that what the language user takes the sign to
mean is a function of his or her purpose and background of
experience at that time. The text and illustration form an open
potential, part of a semiotic data pool, through which the child
constantly generates new hypotheses and discovers new meanings. As young children return to previously read books in collaborative and independent reading situations they are able to
draw on and make use of the sign systems which are meaningful
for them.

Using illustrations to get an overview of meaning and to retrieve meaning

In this example, Sarah's mother reads the whole story of *The
Very Hungry Caterpillar*. Sarah is engrossed in the illustrations,
occasionally murmuring or commenting briefly on an illustration to show she is following along:

Mother: One Sunday morning.
Sarah: Yeah.
Mother: The warm sun came up and – pop! – out of the egg came
a tiny and very hungry caterpillar.
Sarah: Yeh. Nice sun. Big sun.
Mother: He started to look for some food. On Monday he ate
through one apple.
Sarah: Mmm.
Mother: But he was still hungry.
Sarah: Yeh.
Mother: On Tuesday he ate through two pears.

They continued this way through the book, Sarah content to
hear the story and look at the illustrations. Immediately following the shared reading experience Sarah took the book and independently talked her way through a few pages, using the
illustrations as a guide: 'Day. Morning day. Here sun. Big sun.
POP. Here cappa. Cappa look food. Apple, apple, apple. Still
hungry. Pear, pear, pear. Still hungry.'

Expecting all aspects of illustration to contribute to meaning

From the earliest encounters with the books, both children expected all aspects of the illustrations to contribute to the overall meaning. Two-year-old Sarah always 'read' the coloured dots on the title page of *The Very Hungry Caterpillar*. 'Num nums. Nice num nums. Other one num nums,' she would croon as she lovingly ran her fingers across the dots. At the time, the only sweets she was allowed were Smarties, round, multicoloured sweets she called num nums which looked similar in colour and shape to the dots. As the book focused on food, her hypothesis was meaningful as she related her real-life experience to the illustrations.

In a pictorial overview in the beginning of *Rosie's Walk* a tractor is shown beside a barn. Although most of the illustrations from this overview are used again on subsequent pages, the tractor is not. Sarah puzzled about this omission for months, locating the tractor on the overview then searching the other pages for it. Finally, she announced: 'The man must have put the tractor in the shed before Rosie went walking.' Thus satisfactorily accounted for, the tractor was never mentioned again.

Inferring patterns in illustrations that sign meaning

In this next response to the text during a shared reading of *The Very Hungry Caterpillar* Sarah tries to draw her mother's attention to what she sees as a break in an established pattern in the illustrations.

She is concentrating on the five holes that the caterpillar has eaten through the leaf. Each of the foods that the caterpillar has eaten previously has a corresponding number of holes in them (one) and Sarah has perceived this pattern as a consistent sign and is puzzled when it is suddenly broken. Now the text reads 'the caterpillar ate through one nice green leaf' but the illustration shows five holes through the leaf:

> Mother: He ate them all and he was so sick. The next day was Sunday again. The caterpillar ate through one . . .
> Sarah: Piece of 1, 4, 5.

Mother: 5?
Sarah: 1, 2, 6, 11.
Mother: Oh just one.
Sarah: Just one?
Mother: One nice green leaf.
Sarah: 4 there's 1 and 3.
Mother: Pardon?
Sarah: There's 1 and 3.
Mother: Oh, the holes.
Sarah: Yeh.
Mother: 1, 2, 3, 4, 5. There's five holes in the leaf.
Sarah: Yeh.

Harste *et al.* (1984, p. 110) maintain: 'language users assume that the various signs in the literacy event are intentional, non-random and together operate to create a unified meaning.' Clearly, Sarah was actively searching for unity based on her hypothesis and the pattern she had identified as a sign.

Using the illustrations as a scaffold for retelling the story

As Sarah grew in her ability to interpret the language and pictures in books the illustrations provided a scaffold for different interpretations and retellings. When she was reading Tolstoy's version of *The Great Big Enormous Turnip* (1969) she came to the page where the dog was saying something to a cat. The text in the book says, 'The black dog called the cat'. Sarah did her best to get meaning from the text and in her first attempt to interpret the picture she used oral language to represent what she thinks the dog would say to the cat: 'OK. Black dog called the cat and said, "I get off a tree in a minute, a time. I have to get off the tree. I get off." So he got off.' At this period in time Sarah's mother often responded to her with 'Wait a minute. Give me time!' so Sarah's interpretation of the text is very appropriate and fits in with her own experiences.

In Sarah's next version of what the dog was saying to the cat she uses a mixture of oral and story language: 'Black dog called the cat. "Come down now".'

In a final example, Sarah uses story language and retells the story in the exact language of the book: 'The black dog called the cat.'

Using illustrations as intertextual signs

Intertextuality, the process of interpreting current texts by making connections between them and previously read texts, was consistently used as a meaning-making strategy by each child. Perceived links between the illustrations provided a way for Sarah initially to bring meaning to a new book. She has been given a new book, *Ten in the Bed* by Penny Dale (1988), and is looking at the illustrations.

She stops at the page where the animals are all pulling and comments, 'Oooh. Him's like Turnip book!' connecting this illustration to a well-known book *The Great Big Enormous Turnip*. She then proceeds to try out the language structure of the known book on the new book, pointing to each character as she does so: 'Zebra pulled Nellie (*elephant*). Croc pulled Zebra, Teddy pulled Croc, Hedgehog pulled Teddy. They pulled and pulled and couldn't pull him's up.'

In a further example as she is independently revisiting *Harry the Dirty Dog* by Gene Zion (1960), the picture of the bridge across the railway line reminds her of *The Three Billy Goats Gruff*. Her independent reading of this page is: 'Him went up the steps, across the bridge. Trippin' and trappin' across the bridge.' Prompted by the illustration, Sarah is using intertextuality to try on some alternative and quite appropriate language in her retelling of *Harry*. In addition to this, the combination of story language and oral language is also a form of intertextuality that carries meaning for her.

Harste *et al.* (1984, p. 170) suggest that 'from a semiotic perspective, texts sign other texts and hence act as both past and potential texts in their own right'. In each of the preceding samples from the data, meaning has been generated through the interaction which involved the reader's past life and language experiences and the sign complex formed by the print and illustrations, and the situational context.

The evidence from the data suggests that emergent literacy learners not only make connections between past and current texts in the search for meaning but also use the process of intertextuality for the generation of meaning through other communication systems. Intertextuality is then a powerful potential for meaning-making, supporting and sustaining the informant's engagement by providing a network of possible interpretations.

There were three in the bed and the little one said,
"Roll over, roll over!"
So they all rolled over and Bear fell out . . . SLAM!

Ten in the Bed (Dale, 1988)
© P. Dale (1988). Reprinted by permission of the publisher, Walker
Books Ltd., London

Conclusion

Read aloud is an entrenched feature of classroom practice. This
is particularly so in early childhood settings. The use of shared
books which builds on and extends this practice as a foundation
for learning to read also enjoys widespread use.

Evidence from this and other studies which have investigated
repeated rereadings of favourite picture story books (White,

1954; Martinez and Roser, 1985; Sulzby, 1987) provides compelling evidence for their inclusion in literacy learning classrooms. For read aloud and shared books to reach their classroom potential to demonstrate how and why readers read and to engage learners in the process in enjoyable and meaningful ways, children need the opportunity to engage with them repeatedly over time in order to bring their growing cognitive, linguistic and world knowledge to their interpretations. Each opportunity to revisit the books provides the emergent literacy learner with the opportunity not only to confirm and maintain meaning but also to generate new meaning.

The children require shared and independent opportunities to read and reflect, compare and contrast and to experiment with the fittingness of other language and concepts as they innovate on the books to create new versions. Only with time can learners fully utilise the powerful meaning-making strategy of intertextuality as they make links between characters, language, plots, story structures, illustrative features and styles, and their life and language experiences to arrive at meaning and to generate further meaning.

Learners also need the opportunity to read for a variety of purposes. Rereading a book for a particular purpose such as thinking like the author and considering why the author chose a particular topic or chose specific language to convey the message, or alternatively, to consider what suggestions the author may have given the illustrator, demonstrate ways of taking new perspectives of familiar materials. In this way reading continues to be demonstrated and shared as a thinking, transactive process, an open potential in which the readers play an active role.

Bibliography

Baghban, M. (1984) *Our Daughter Learns to Read and Write: A Case Study from Birth to Three.* Newark, Del: International Reading Association.

Brown, M. (1957) *The Three Billy Goats Gruff*, New York: Harcourt.

Burningham, J. (1977) *Come away from the Water, Shirley.* London: Jonathan Cape.

Carle, E. (1974) *The Very Hungry Caterpillar.* Harmondsworth: Puffin.

Cochran-Smith, M. (1984) *The Making of a Reader.* Norwood, NJ: Ablex.

Dale, P. (1988) *Ten in the Bed.* London: Walker Books.

Dombey, H. (1989) Learning the language of books. In Meek, M. (ed), *Opening Moves.* London: Bedford Way Papers.

Durkin, D. (1966) *Children who Read Early.* New York: Teachers College Press.

Gilman, P. (1992) *Something from Nothing*, Ontario: North Winds Press.

Harste, J., Woodward, V. and Burke, C. (1984) *Language Stories and Literacy Lessons.* Portsmouth, NH: Heinemann.

Holdaway, D. (1979) *The Foundations of Literacy.* Sydney: Ashton Scholastic.

Huey, E.D. (1908) *The Psychology and Pedagogy of Reading.* Cambridge, Mass.: MIT Press (reprinted in 1973).

Hutchins, P. (1969) *Rosie's Walk.* London: Bodley Head.

Martinez, M. and Roser, N. (1985) Read it again: the value of repeated reading during storytime, *The Reading Teacher*, Vol. 38, 782–6.

Parkes, B.J. (1990) Case study explorations of emergent literacy learners' transactions with picture story books. Unpublished doctoral thesis. University of Wollongong.

Sulzby, E. (1987) Children's emergent reading of favourite storybooks: a developmental study, *Reading Research Quarterly*, 20, 458–81.

Tolstoy, A. (1969) *The Great Big Enormous Turnip*. Harmondsworth: Puffin.

Wells, C.G. (1982) Story reading and the development of symbolic skills, *Australian Journal of Reading*, Vol. 5, 142–52.

White, D.N. (1954) *Books before five*. Portsmouth, NH: Heinemann.

Yaden, D.B. (1988) Understood stories through repeated read alouds: how many does it take? *Reading Teacher*, Vol. 41, 556–60.

Zion, G. (1960) *Harry the Dirty Dog*. London: Bodley Head.

Chapter 4

Linking books to develop older children's response to literature

Pam Baddeley and Chris Eddershaw

In this chapter we explore how older children's response to literature can be developed through linking picture books which have a common theme. This idea arose for us out of some work with children on traditional and modern stories involving stepmothers (Baddeley and Eddershaw, 1994). Viewing the stepmother theme from different angles appeared to enable the children to gain deeper insights into the individual books and to develop their thinking about stepmothers in general. This discovery interested us and appeared to hold useful possibilities for further work with children.

This approach differs from the more conventional one where picture books are often loosely linked to a topic and used as a starting point, e.g. 'Water' or 'Homes'. Whilst this is a legitimate approach it often fails to exploit the potential of picture books for older children from a literary and artistic point of view. Through our previous work we were aware of the potential of picture books to stimulate interest and discussion among older children. The interplay of text and pictures enabled them to read the subtext and to gain insights into character and the important themes underlying the often amusing and light-hearted stories: 'Because of their special accessibility, they give the child an early encounter with what literature on its own will effect later' (Graham, J., 1990, p. 84).

We chose a selection of picture books which were more subtly linked in the hope that the children would discover the underlying theme linking the books. We presented the children with this challenge right from the beginning so that in the process of discovering that link they would initially be involved in interpretation of the texts and pictures, and then might see similarities in those interpretations; finally, they might make some general statements about what appeared to be the linking theme. We also hoped that this process of exploration of a very varied selection of picture books with a common theme would deepen their understanding of human behaviour and the role of the author/illustrator. In discussing Thomson's (1987) 'Developmental model of reader-response to literature', Michaels and Walsh (1990, p. 42) comment that:

> The picture book is a medium with which a teacher can develop those later stages of reader-response, particularly with those 'reluctant' readers of novels. Readers can be led through a 'shared book' approach – whether on a teacher-class level or peer-group level – to enjoy the story, to feel with characters, to respond to and evaluate the ideas, and to develop critical perceptions about the implied author in the picture book. The use of certain picture books can not only be applicable to particular stages but can help to move readers to other stages of reader response.

The books we chose appeared to us to have a common link: characters who are unable to, or have difficulty in seeing another person's point of view. Over a period of several weeks the teacher read the books with the children and discussed each one in turn. The mixed-ability group of 10-year-old children (six boys and two girls) included two children who were statemented. (It is worth noting that Tom and Paul both made significant contributions to the discussions.) The group was gradually encouraged to think about what the books might have in common, but a real consideration of this was left until all the books had been read. It became evident that the children found identifying the link that we had made quite difficult. However, they came up with a variety of their own, one of which was particularly applicable; so just because they did not easily identify our link did not negate the value of the process.

As the discussions progressed other important aspects of the children's learning became apparent. They pored over the pictures with enormous pleasure and as a result developed their ability to understand their significance; and they were able to infer meaning from the pictures which was not always contained in the text. With the help of the teacher they also advanced their skills of discussion. They expanded their ideas through listening to and challenging each other, demanding evidence, presenting ideas logically and beginning to summarise their positions.

> The teacher or other adult can encourage the children to venture into new areas of understanding, to deepen their response, to grasp at things only dimly perceived, to talk about the meaning of the book itself. The opportunities for personal growth are great, and those for language development are perhaps even greater (Fremantle, 1993, p. 12).

What follows is an attempt to indicate how the children responded initially to each of the six books, and how in the final discussion they generalised about possible links between them.

Cousin Blodwyn's Visit (Vesey, 1983)

Capillaris is a witch whose unpleasant habits and hygene are what you would expect of a witch. Her forceful cousin Blodwyn invites herself to stay and, despite Capillaris' wishes, cleans up the house and garden to suit her own standards.

After reading this first book, the children initially supplied a moral for the story in response to the teacher's question:

> Teacher: So what's, what's this book really about then? What's going on underneath the story?
> Roger: About keeping things tidy and just trying to make an effort.

The children then appeared to contradict that message by arguing that Cousin Blodwyn was wrong to try to change Cousin Capillaris because Capillaris was brought up in the tradition of witches to be untidy:

> Teacher: So Cousin Blodwyn is completely wrong to try to change Cousin Capillaris – is she?
> Tom/Roger: Yes.
> Teacher: Roger, why do you think that?
> Roger: Well that's just how she is I think.
> Jeff: She was brought up that way and so she should be left that way.
> Paul: And witches are meant to be untidy anyway.

That viewpoint led Kevin, another child, to suggest that Cousin Blodwyn was failing to think about other people. She thought about them in the sense that she imagined that what they needed was to be tidied up and that she was, therefore, actually trying to be kind even if she did not succeed in being so. Owen expanded on this idea:

> Owen: There's like two kinds – tidy people and messy people. She's one of the tidy people and some people like it tidy and some people don't. So what she does she wants to help . . . she's kind of being kind . . . willing to help her tidy it up but she can't – she's not actually invited so she . . . there's no point in her really doing it 'cos (*interrupted*) –
> Tom: She's trying to be kind in heart.
> Owen: She's trying to be kind but
> Kevin: It's not working.

Libby, however, swiftly shifted their interpretation into a different gear by interrupting that conversation to say, emphatically, that Cousin Blodwyn was acting on purely selfish grounds:

> Libby: I don't think Cousin Blodwyn is trying to be kind because she's just trying to make everything better for herself. She was trying to make the house nice for *her*. She wasn't trying to be kind to her cousin, she just wanted it to be how she wanted it.
> Kevin: How *she* wanted it.

During the course of this conversation the children had regularly pored over the illustrations, fascinated and amused by the changing details. That interest culminated in a perceptive insight from Tom and Owen, which the teacher acknowledged and deliberately summarised to underline the point:

> Tom: All the cats are happy now.
> Teacher (*laughing*): Yes, they are, they are.
> Owen: The cats kind of tell a story 'cos when Cousin Blodwyn's there it's all tidy and they look really sad, but when she's gone they can get back to normal so they are happy.
> Teacher: Yes, that's a super comment Owen. He's noticed in the detail, by just looking at the pictures, the pictures tell a story in even greater detail than the text about the cats 'cos the cats look very apprehensive when they see Cousin Blodwyn at the beginning don't they, and then they get very unhappy as they are all lined up smartly and very clean looking – they're afraid of her aren't they – in the kitchen. But now, at the end, they're looking happy – so, as Owen said, the cats tell a story too.

Cousin Blodwyn's Visit (Vesey, 1983)
Reprinted from *Cousin Blodwyn's Visit* © 1983 by A. Vesey, with permission of Methuen Children's Books.

In the course of this first discussion one of the children offered an interpretation of the meaning of the book. This was challenged by the others and in the process of this discussion the behaviour and motives of the characters were analysed. The children 'read' the pictures and gleaned additional information from them.

Crusher is Coming! (Graham, B., 1990)

Peter, the little boy in the story, invites home his new friend Crusher. He has plans for the afternoon which do not include his small sister Claire but which he hopes will interest Crusher. Despite his name and tough appearance, and contrary to Peter's expectations, Crusher willingly joins in Claire's tea party and other games. Peter finds it hard to involve Crusher in his plans and Crusher and the afternoon turn out different from his expectations.

In discussing this book, the children were able to empathise with Peter and the situation in which he found himself when he

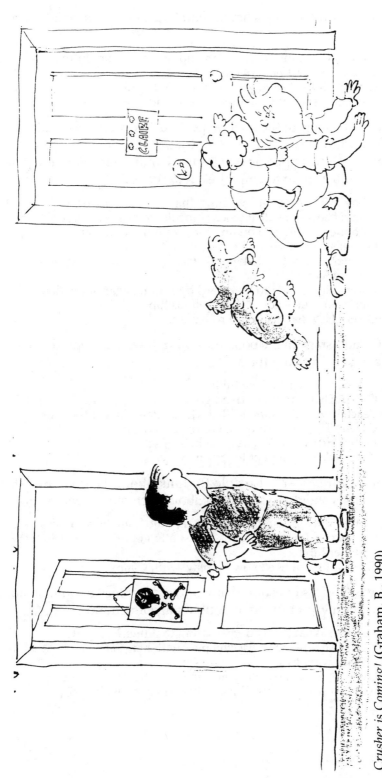

Crusher is Coming! (Graham, B., 1990)
Reprinted from B. Graham (1990) *Crusher is Coming* by permission of Lothian Books

arrived home with his new friend Crusher whom he intended to impress:

> Libby: His mum's kissing him and he's going bright red.
> Owen: He must be *very* embarrassed.
> Kevin: Like when my granny came round – *very, very* embar-rassed! – especially about what she said.

At a later stage in the book when Crusher continues to play with Peter's little sister (see p. 63), Claire, the children again made links with their personal experience and interpreted the details of the illustration to empathise with Peter:

> Libby: He's probably wishing that Crusher hadn't come . . . I would because I hate it when someone comes to my house to play with me and they go off and play with my brothers.
> Owen: You can see it in his face.
> Teacher: Right, the look on his face . . . Anything else about him in that picture?
> Owen: He's trying to look hard by leaning against the door.
> Libby: And he's got his hand on his hip.
> Owen: He's got his sleeve rolled up.

At a later stage in the book the children were interpreting Peter's feelings by reading the subtext:

> Teacher: So what's Pete thinking?
> Owen: That's another friend gone!
> Teacher: Aha (*laughing*) What's he actually saying though?
> Owen: 'Thanks for buying her the ice-cream.'
> Libby: He's not like letting on he's upset.
> Kevin: He's trying not to give it away.

The children were also able to think about the book by asking questions about the story and about each other's comments:

> Libby: Why doesn't Pete just try and join in and play with Crusher and Claire . . . 'cos he usually got on – he usually plays with her I think? . . .
> Owen: How do we know he plays with Claire?

It was Owen's question that led to a difference of opinion about how to interpret the final double-page illustration:

> Teacher: What can you 'read' from that then?
> Kevin: That he does (*usually*) play with her (*Claire*) except that he doesn't want to show it to Crusher.
> Owen: No . . . how do you know 'cos he could like be playing with her *now* because Crusher liked playing with her?

Crusher is Coming! (Graham, B., 1990)
Reprinted from B. Graham (1990) *Crusher is Coming* by permission of Lothian Books

However, the children did not (nor, unfortunately, did the teacher lead them to) generalise about what might be underlying the story – that Peter imposed on Crusher, his mother and sister, his view of Crusher and, possibly, that Peter wasn't being true to his own character with the result that he got left out of things until the end of the book.

During the course of this second discussion the children empathised with the characters through relating to their own experience; they read the subtext; they questioned the text and each other and they argued about the interpretation of the pictures.

Julius, the Baby of the World (Henkes, 1994)

Lilly thinks her new baby brother is disgusting. In spite of her parents' loving attempts to help her accept him, she does all she can to express her jealousy in a variety of imaginative ways. However, when Cousin Garland also expresses dislike of Julius, Lilly rapidly changes her mind about her brother.

In the discussion of this book the children appreciated the parents' as well as Lilly's point of view with regard to Lilly's jealousy of her baby brother. In interpreting the picture Paul deduced and empathised with Lilly's feelings and commented on the parents' apparent failings. Tom and Roger's counter-argument, however, is based on evidence from the text:

> Paul: She's feeling left out 'cos look at her she's sitting on a stool and they're up there . . . she looks upset . . . I reckon they should pay more attention to her.
> Tom: I don't 'cos when *she* was young she got the same attention . . .
> Paul: *She* reckons that she should get all the attention . . .
> Roger: They try and tell her that they want to, the mother and the father are trying to tell her that they want the baby to be just like her, so she should admire that . . . they're trying to spend some time with her but they've got to look after the baby, but she doesn't want the baby.

That last point led to Tom's unsolicited and astute comment: 'Lilly will only be happy when everybody hates Julius.' Tom's comment was taken up later when Libby questioned exactly what Lilly had against her baby brother: 'What's he supposed to have done?' Libby's question led to the children making explicit their thoughts about Julius who, to the parents, was 'the baby of the world' and, to his sister, was 'disgusting':

Paul: (*The baby's*) Quite nice, but Lilly doesn't think so.
Kevin: It's cute.

The children began to feel that Lilly's problem was, ultimately, the fault of the parents for not sitting down with Lilly to talk things through, a feeling supported by Tom's very perceptive insight into Lilly's motives:

And she is sort of like . . . it's the parents' fault but she is . . . the only way she can get back on the parents . . . she can't really pull faces at the parents and do magic on them 'cos they would just straightaway . . . so she does it on the baby which is the nearest thing to the parents . . . so she can do the next best thing.

However, the implied suggestion that Lilly might change her mind about Julius if only her parents would sit down and talk with her was questioned by some of the children:

Teacher: Why wouldn't it make much difference, Jeff?
Jeff: Because she . . . it wouldn't make much difference to the baby (*i.e. the baby would still be around*).
Paul: Because if they sat down and talked to her she wouldn't care . . . she wouldn't be listening.
Libby: She's just determined to be difficult. She's doesn't want to make life easy for anyone . . . she's just determined to be difficult.

The problem of what to do about someone who is unable or unwilling to see another point of view is one that Lilly herself has to face when Cousin Garland comes to the celebration Lilly's parents hold in honour of Julius. Lilly has her own way of making Cousin Garland adopt her point of view, a technique the teacher suggested to the children that the parents might have employed with Lilly:

Teacher: So . . . the way to help someone overcome those feelings (*of jealousy*) is to tell them, is it?
Kevin: Um . . . yeah . . . sometimes.
Jeff: It depends . . .
Kevin: It doesn't always work.
Tom: It depends if you're forcing them or not.
Teacher: What is Lilly doing, Owen, to Cousin Garland?
Owen: Make . . . yeh. Forcing her to like him . . .
Tom: Cousin Garland still doesn't probably like him (*Julius*) but she's afraid to say she doesn't now.

During this discussion it was obvious that the children understood that there were two points of view about Julius but had not identified this as an underlying theme.

It was at this point that the teacher gave the children their first opportunity to explore possible links between some of the books read so far:

> Teacher: Is there any link between this book and *Cousin Blodwyn's Visit*, I wonder?
> Paul: No, none.
> Kevin: There is because Cousin Blodwyn and Julius are about the same (*interrupted*).
> Roger: Yeah . . . er . . . 'cos in *Cousin Blodwyn* . . . Cousin Capillaris didn't like Cousin Blodwyn and it's the same sort of thing in this book.
> Kevin: That Lilly didn't like Julius.
> Tom: In this book yeah . . . but in this book (*Julius*) they got used to it but in that book they didn't.
> Libby: In those books they were trying to make people do what they didn't want to do . . . 'cos Lilly's parents were trying to make her like Julius and . . . Cousin Blodwyn was trying to make Capillaris tidy up the house and things and she didn't want to.

There appears to be a movement in their analysis from simply identifying surface similarities to making a generalisation about the characters' behaviour which may link two of the books together.

William's Doll (Zolotow and Pene du Bois, 1985)

William wants a doll. His brother and friend ridicule him, and his father gives him toys which he thinks are more suitable. These William enjoys but he still wants a doll. His grandmother understands and buys him one and explains to his father that he needs one in order to practise being a successful father.

The fourth book aroused just the sexist attitude of which it is critical. However, despite their incredulity and ridicule which mirrored the reactions of some of the characters, the children did make a distinction between the socially accepted norm and moral values:

> Teacher: You seem to be saying it's not normal . . . it's odd for this boy to be wanting a doll (*interrupted*).
> Philip: Weird.
> Teacher: It's weird . . . is it then . . . is it . . . is it not natural?
> Jeff: It's not natural.
> Kevin: It's not that natural but there's nothing wrong.

Libby took that point a step further by suggesting that age is an important factor in affecting the judgements people make concerning what is/is not socially acceptable: 'It depends how old he is because um my little brother used to play with dolls when he was about 3 or 4 and, um, now he doesn't because he's older . . . so it depends how old you are.'

Paul mentioned Action Man for older boys but that point was disregarded because it clearly was not the kind of doll that William wanted. In order to challenge their thinking the teacher told the children that, when he was at school in Wales, several of the boys were keen on football but were afraid to play it because it was sneered at as being a woman's game, whereas rugby was regarded as the game that men played. That anecdote not surprisingly stung the children, especially the boys, so Kevin at least was able to take the children's thinking a stage further through his response to the teacher's question:

Teacher: Who's saying that these things are what men do, what women do?
Kevin: The people themselves.

Exactly who those 'people' are and why they, perhaps, make such judgements was not really explored, but the discussion did lead to Roger putting up a brave defence for the individual and to Libby's further comment taking on board Roger's suggestion and questioning the text in the process:

Roger: Why can't you let the *person* decide what they want to do?
Libby: If he wants a doll then he can have a doll . . . Why doesn't his dad just go out and buy him a doll?

The other children had no difficulty in empathising with the father's concern for William if he did buy him a doll:

Kevin: (*The father thinks* . . .) That he's going to be a *girl*.
Owen: That he's going to get teased, bullied and he's going to get a very black eye.

The children were able to infer how the Grandmother might view William's father:

Kevin: He's not thinking.
Libby: He's just a normal father.

However, they were less sympathetic to the grandmother's suggestion that having a doll to play with would make William a better father. Owen: 'No, it's just – that won't make him a better father, it's just like making him more – make him happy instead of he doesn't get too grumpy so he just like stops everything.'

The children's final position seemed to be expressed by Jeff: 'If he wants a doll he can have a doll but he'll have to put up with being teased.' However, Roger appeared to be questioning the social assumptions that the other children were taking for granted: 'The thing is . . . it's not strange for a girl to do a boy's thing but it's strange for a boy to want to do a girl's thing.' During this discussion the children were much more concerned with the apparently unconventional behaviour of the main character than with the more general issues posed by the book. However, the children, through empathising with the characters, referring to personal experience and developing each other's ideas, moved beyond their initially rigid stance.

Mole Moves House (Buchanan and Buchanan, 1989)

Mole, seeing him dig his vegetables, recognises that Mr Carrington is as good a digger as himself. Mole decides to become his neighbour and help him with his digging. Mr Carrington does not appreciate the mole hills in his garden and thinks up some ingenious ways to get rid of him. Each of these Mole turns to own advantage, apparently not recognising the implied lack of gratitude for his help. The Carringtons, when nothing appears to deter Mole, decide to move. Mole, feeling himself to be a valued member of the family, knows he is needed in the new garden and goes with them.

The humour of this book lies in the use of irony, particularly in the way in which the narrator tells the story from the Mole's point of view, suggesting his complete inability to see Mr Carrington's frustration and anger at his 'help'.

The children fairly soon identified this humour in the language and, with the teacher's prompting, were able to explain it:

> Teacher (*reading*): 'He could tell that Mr Carrington was surprised' (*some of children beginning to laugh*). Why did you have a little laugh to yourselves there?
> Tom: Because he was probably . . . Mole thought he was surprised in a different way.

Teacher (*laughing*): Yes . . . you sort of gave a hint of what Mr Carrington might be thinking . . . what might he be thinking there?
Kevin: 'I'll KILL you!'

They also showed that they were increasingly aware of the contradiction between the text and the pictures, between what Mole thought Mr Carrington was thinking and what Mr Carrington was actually thinking:

Teacher (*reading*): 'He would relax with his family, trusting that Mole would do a quality job in the garden.' Who's writing that?
Tom: The narrator – he's sort of trying to make it sound like he's happy but then the picture . . . (*interrupted*).

The teacher's question about the text also led the children to identify the narrator's ironic use of language and led them to use irony for themselves:

Kevin: No, Mole is, um, Mole's thinking, um, he's writing what Mole is thinking.
Teacher: And what does Mole think?
Kevin: He's helping Mr Carrington.
Tom: Mole's telling the story.
Teacher: Yes, and what does Mole think Mr Carrington is thinking?
Jeff: It's a really, really good job.
Tom: Brilliant job!
Teacher: Yes, a brilliant job!
Tom: I really wanted my garden dug up and all messy, and I didn't want any grass.

The children appeared to have glimpsed the structure of the book: the way the narration, the contradiction between the pictures and the text, the economic use of some of the language all work together to underline the irony of the situation:

Tom: The man's telling the story by pictures but the Mole's telling the story by . . .
Kevin: Writing.

During the discussion about how Mole seems incapable of realising what other people are thinking about him, Owen suddenly interjected with a reference to *Cousin Blodwyn's Visit*: 'It's like Cousin Blodwyn, Mole's come when he's not wanted.' Here, Owen is spontaneously making a link between two of the books at the level of characterisation.

Fun (Mark and Foreman, 1987)

James enjoys quietly observing the wonders of his small world. His exuberant parents want him to play with them and constantly unthinkingly interrupt his absorption in natural objects and events in order to interest him in more active pursuits.

The final book the children looked at was *Fun*. They did see the distinction between the way the little boy, James, likes to behave and the way his mother does:

> Libby: She likes to be really lively . . . he likes to be quiet.
> Tom: She wants to make him happy like her.

Although they recognised that distinction early on in their reading of the book they did not appear to appreciate that the parents, particularly the mother, seems anxious to try to play with James by encouraging him to do the things young children traditionally find fun. Rather, they thought of them as odd, peculiar, even crazy towards the end of the book despite admitting that parents should play with their children:

> Tom: Normal mums don't do stuff like that, do they – they go up to you and say 'What are you looking at?' and stuff like that.
> Libby: They try to make you quiet.
> Teacher: Oh, so normal mums don't play with their children?
> Tom: Yeah, they do . . . but they don't go out and jump in puddles and stuff.
> Libby: Usually it's kids who jump in puddles and mums try and stop them.

The children did realise at different points in the book that the parents find it hard to appreciate that James is not having fun doing the things they think he would enjoy:

> Libby: James' mum says that they have a lot of fun at home – *she* does, James doesn't . . .
> Tom: *She* thinks he's having fun . . .
> Tom: She thinks it's making him happy.
> Paul: Yes, you'd have thought that she'd have noticed by now that it isn't making him happy.

The children fleetingly empathised with the parents' feelings when James announces that he wants to go to the playschool:

> Teacher: What do you think James' parents are thinking at that moment?

Fun (Mark and Foreman, 1987)
Illustration by Michael Foreman from *Fun* by Jan Mark (Victor Gollancz/
Hamish Hamilton, 1987). Copyright © Michael Foreman, 1987.

> Tom: They're starting to get a bit sad.
> Jeff: He's not like them.

However, despite their critical judgement of the parents, the
children ignored for a long time the fact that Michael Foreman
had illustrated the mother and the father, at bath time, holding a
toy crocodile and a shark in their hands until Libby made the
following observation:

> Libby: The parents are a bit like the shark and the crocodile.
> Teacher: What made you say that?
> Libby: 'Cos they're sort of rough.
> Roger: They can't leave James in peace for one minute.

That led Roger to make this comment and Jeff to make the first
attempt to link all the books:

> Roger: This book is like the one last week – the mole one – leave
> me alone – and that's what this one is about.
> Jeff: All these books are saying 'Get away from me I don't want you'.

As with the other books, the children had continued to make
perceptive comments about characters and behaviour, relating

the book to their own experience. However, this discussion also included that leap forward when Jeff spontaneously linked together all the books.

Final discussion

Until now, the children had mainly focused on the meaning of each individual book. When the children were finally asked to discuss what they thought linked the books they put forward a range of ideas which were then applied to each of the books in turn to see if they were valid. The first idea that emerged was that in each of the books the expectations of the reader were not fulfilled. Libby:

> The people are all different from how you would expect them to be because like James' parents in *Fun* you wouldn't expect parents to be like that . . . and, um, Cousin Blodwyn is a witch but she doesn't act like one . . . and, um, Mr Carrington was doing all that stuff to Mole and you would have thought Mole would have hated it. In all the books it's like, um, and you would expect Crusher to sort of be hard and not all play with little children and that, um, he does play with little children . . . they're all like you would expect them not to be.

This was a sophisticated and sustained piece of thinking on Libby's part; she had not only come up with a valid idea but had also begun spontaneously to apply it to the books. Unfortunately, before she had a chance to refer to *William's Doll* and *Julius, the Baby of the World*, Paul ventured another idea:

> Paul: They all want to be different . . . (*interrupted*).
> Teacher: Wait a moment . . . just carry on Paul . . . they all want to be different . . . can you just explain that?
> Paul: In *Julius, the Baby of the World*, Lilly the big sister's different. She wanted to be different. When she found out that someone else didn't like the baby she changed, didn't she?
> Kevin: I disagree on that.

Again a further idea was introduced before that difference of opinion had been resolved:

> Jeff: And, um, all the books is like they don't want them to be there.
> Teacher: Hold on, we've got a new theory coming forward that what links the books is?
> Tom: They all want to be left alone.

That theory was then applied to five of the books and culminated in the following exchange which was concluded by Roger momentarily adopting the teacher's role and clarifying, and slightly developing, the other children's ideas through a general statement:

> Teacher: Now what about *William's Doll*?
> Cathy: It's the same with that one 'cos . . .
> Tom: Yeah, he wants his dad to . . .
> Libby: He wants them to stop teasing him.
> Kevin: No . . . he wants his brothers to go away because he doesn't want them to tease him.
> Tom: Yeah, and he wants his dad to go away so he can get the doll.
> Roger: We're saying here that people want to live their own life, that they do what they want to do.

In thinking about why certain characters in the books did not allow others to be themselves, the children came up with another idea and the teacher encouraged further analysis:

> Kevin: They're thinking, um, all the books are connected by their thinking they're helping but they're not (*helping*).
> Teacher: Um, right, some characters in the book think that they are helping but in fact they're not. Well, let's test it out . . . does that theory work with *Fun*?
> Voices: Yeah, yes, yes.
> Teacher: Right, talk it through then . . . why does it work with *Fun*?

They then discussed *Fun* and several of the other books. Having to apply a general theory encouraged the children to wrestle with their thoughts about each particular book. In referring to *William's Doll*, Tom made a contribution which seemed to be a good example of what Barnes (1992, p. 126) referred to as exploratory talk: 'Exploratory talk is often hesitant and incomplete; it enables the speaker to try ideas, to hear how they sound, to see what others make of them, to arrange information and ideas into different patterns.'

Tom appears to think his way through to a reason for the dad's motives and behaviour, thoughts that were not expressed in the original discussion of that book:

> His dad probably thinks he's helping because he . . . to make sure so if one of his friends finds out he doesn't get teased . . . it's sort

of like . . . that's why he doesn't want to buy him a doll 'cos he might get teased so that's why 'cos he'd have to, I mean . . . um, he doesn't want him to get teased that's why he's not buying him a doll and he's trying to make up to him by buying him all that other stuff.

The teacher's idea of what linked the books – characters who have difficulty in seeing another person's point of view – was raised by the children but only briefly discussed. Then the teacher invited what he thought might be a pertinent contribution from Libby:

> Teacher: Come on then Libby, Libby's been desperate to say something about this 'point of view'.
> Libby: No, it's not really about that . . . I think that in these stories everyone needs to just sit down and talk and they're not doing that . . . if they did they could sort a lot of stuff out but they just . . . they're just trying to sort things out the wrong way.

Despite the quality of that contribution the teacher still tried to focus on 'points of view'. However, after further discussion Kevin returned to Libby's idea which quickly led her to summarise the connection between these ideas (i.e. lack of talk; therefore people don't understand each other; therefore they do not behave in an appropriate way):

> Teacher: Right, well we'll come to the point that Kevin's taking up from what Libby said – that the characters fail to talk to each other about these things – Libby?
> Libby: People aren't – they can't think what someone else is thinking so they don't know what they're going through and they can't really understand . . . so they just guess . . . that's the problem in the end.
> Teacher: Right . . . yes . . . so they fail to talk to each other so they can't really understand . . .
> Libby: People can't understand each other.
> Teacher: Right . . . they don't talk therefore they don't understand each other.
> Libby: And they don't know what the other person's going through and they're trying to help in the wrong way.
> Teacher: Yes . . . because they don't talk they don't understand each other and they are actually helping in the wrong way.

Having established that lack of communication might be a linking factor, the teacher encouraged the children to think about what effect this had on the characters, particularly Peter in *Crusher is Coming!*:

Teacher: So what is the effect, this is what I'm trying to take you beyond – recognising what's going on in the book to looking a little bit deeper – what is the effect ultimately upon the characters in these books, and we're just taking Peter as an example?
Libby: That he should be his own person like Crusher.
Tom: Don't try and pretend that he's not that person.
Libby: He should be just who he is.
Kevin: Stop pretending, be who he is.

This was a further illustration of how encouraging children to make general statements and to justify them can deepen their thinking about those books.

Conclusion

It became obvious that the value of these discussions lay not necessarily in the discovery of the teacher's idea but in the journey that the children made in coming to their own conclusions and having to justify them. As Chambers (1993, p. 43) commented: 'In telling their readings they activate their potentialities, but only when that reading is truly their own and is co-operatively shared, and is not someone else's reading imposed upon them.'

The excitement and pleasure older children experience when they discover for themselves the unexpected depths of good-quality picture books we have always found rewarding. As one of the children said: 'These books are like baby books but if you look at them carefully you can turn them into something else.' Older children's involvement with the characters, their interpretation of the pictures, their appreciation of the language and their reading of the subtext all indicated to us the undoubted value of this type of book. Our impression was again confirmed by this group's initial discussions of the individual books. However, the cumulative effect of linking a group of books and the final discussion in which the children had to generalise and hold up their ideas for scrutiny, added a new dimension. The careful choice of subtly linked books, the teacher's support during the discussion and the process this took the children through were all important aspects of the approach. In the light of our experience, we would strongly recommend any teacher, who has not already done so, to experiment with linking picture books in this particular way.

Bibliography

Baddeley, P. and Eddershaw, C. (1994) *Not So Simple Picture Books: Developing Responses to Literature with 4–12 Year Olds*, Stoke-on-Trent: Trentham Books.

Barnes, D. (1992) The role of talk in learning. In Norman, K. *et al.* (eds.) *Thinking Voices*, London, Sydney and Auckland: Hodder & Stoughton.

Buchanan, E. and Buchanan, G. (1989) *Mole Moves House*, London: Macdonald Children's Books.

Chambers, A. (1993) *Tell Me: Children, Reading and Talk*, Stroud: Thimble Press.

Fremantle, S. (1993) The power of the picture book. In Pinsent, P. *et al.* (eds.) *The Power of the Page: Children's Books and their Readers*, London: David Fulton.

Graham, B. (1990) *Crusher is Coming!* London: Collins Picture Lions.

Graham, J. (1990) *Pictures on the Page*, Sheffield: NATE.

Henkes, K. (1994) *Julius, the Baby of the World*, Harmondsworth: Picture Puffins.

Mark, J. and Foreman, M. (1987) *Fun*, London: Victor Gollancz.

Michaels, W. and Walsh, M. (1990) *Up and Away: Using Picture Books*, Melbourne: Oxford University Press.

Thompson, J. (1987) *Understanding Teenagers' Reading; Reading Processes and the Teaching of Literature*, Sydney: Methuen Australia.

Vesey, A. (1983) *Cousin Blodwyn's Visit*, London: Methuen Children's Books.

Zolotow, C. and Pene du Bois, W. (1985) *William's Doll*, New York: Harper Trophy.

Chapter 5

A way into a new language and culture
Liz Laycock

I met Iqbal, briefly, on the day he arrived in the reception class in a Tower Hamlets school. He was brought by the headteacher to meet his class, holding very tightly to her hand and looking amazed and bewildered in these new surroundings. He spoke Sylheti (a Bengali dialect) and was completely new to English. The school was one which was accustomed to this situation and Iqbal was warmly welcomed by his teacher using her very few words of his language. For the rest of the day he watched and listened, but did not speak. I saw him again three weeks later when I joined the class half way through the morning. He was utterly engrossed in play with construction materials, smiling and pleased with his achievement. But it was almost break time, and very soon the teacher stopped the children and announced 'It's clearing-up time'. Iqbal stopped immediately, looked up, beaming even more widely and echoed, 'clear-up time'! He set about clearing away his materials and then proceeded to help all those around him to put away the things they were using, repeating 'clear-up time' to each person or group. He was clearly delighted by his understanding of what was required and by his ability to participate in the activity. His teacher told me that this phrase had been the first (and only) English he had spoken so far and that he repeated the phrase every time it was used!

This snapshot demonstrates vividly two, if not three, of the essential conditions identified by Krashen and Terrell (1983) for the successful acquisition of a new language:

1) Comprehensible input.
2) A stress-free environment.
3) The right to silence.

Iqbal had been shown from the start that his language was valued, so the stress level was decreased; the clearing-up routine
and the language which went with it was comprehensible because it was accompanied by actions he could see and make
sense of; and he felt able to use the appropriate language because he understood it and wanted to speak, not because he was
being made to speak.

The young child who is new to English must make sense of a
whole new world (Gregory, 1996) when he or she arrives in
school. All children starting school must learn to become pupils.
They must learn what the expectations are when they are in a
group of thirty or more children with one or two adults; this
new environment has rules and customs which are often different from the ways of behaving in the world outside school
(for example, lining up, answering the register, new forms of
address, daily routines) and they must seem strange and often
bizarre! This is true, too, for the older child, who may already
have become accustomed to other routines of school in a different cultural context. Indeed, cultural expectations of schools
and schooling may also be very different. For the child who is
new to English, all this must be accomplished despite having
little or no understanding of the words the teacher is using, so
gestures, visual and practical support become crucial, as do opportunities to talk (in either language) and to try out the new
language without fear of making mistakes.

At the same time as he or she is coming to terms with the
classroom environment, the child must make a start on acquiring the skills of literacy. This is where, if the teacher approaches
teaching in a way which both draws on the child's out-of-school
experiences and demonstrates the pleasures and purposes of
reading, the child with English as an additional language need
not be disadvantaged. It is almost a cliché to say that teaching
approaches which are good for learners new to English are good
for all learners, but it is true that many monolingual learners
have the same needs as those new to English. The rich resource
of picture books, if well chosen and used in carefully structured

ways, provides the additional support that is needed. The child who is new to English does not have to depend solely on the written text when there are visual clues to support and extend understanding.

For readers new to English, whether or not they are literate in another language, the textless picture book is often the ideal starting point because the whole story is in the pictures, which can be interpreted uniquely by each reader. In the following extract from a session with *The Gift* by John Prater (1985), two children, Syrihah (a girl, 6;4, who is new to school in England and not yet able to communicate in English) and Nazmul (a boy, 5;9, who is beginning to use some English) are working with a support teacher. They have looked through the book with her and she has talked, in English, about what is happening. The teacher then invites the children to tell the story; Syrihah tells the story in Sylheti and Nazmul tells in English. At the beginning Nazmul gives the boy and girl characters their two names:

Nazmul: It's *The Gift*. One day my, no, Syrihah and Nazmul (*names*) . . . box . . . gift . . . he open too hard . . . he found two chair . . . yellow chair . . . (pp. 1–2).
Syrihah: (*telling*).
Nazmul: OK . . . there she's open but he out chair . . . two chairs he good aren't they . . . see they in the chair.
Syrihah: (*telling*).
Nazmul: Is good – I go now (*referring to his turn*) he's . . . he broke . . . an' broke. He sit down in the . . . Nazmul said get off . . . get to me . . . I too big, too . . . It's your turn (*to Syrihah*).
Syrihah: (*telling*).
Nazmul: Syrihah said look I can fly up . . . his open his eye and said look Syrihah, I can fly – it's your turn (*to Syrihah*).
Syrihah: (*telling*) (pp. 3–4).
Nazmul: The she, he crash, a (*pause*) . . . a big truck and car . . . Nazmul said (*squeaking noise and covering eyes as in picture*) . . . he scared he . . . Syrihah is scared. Then she go to trainway, um, er, tunnel . . . there she is, look . . . hello said . . . we whisshhh (*noise of whizzing by*) . . . your turn.
Syrihah: (*telling*) (pp, 5–6).
Nazmul: There she's go to, er (*looking to teacher for help*) . . . go in the . . .
Teacher: Station.
Nazmul: The station . . . his dog ruff, ruff, ruff . . . look in book . . . he dog, look, ruff, ruff, ruff said dog . . . he walk in the tunnel . . . he dark . . . he scared. I'm scared said the Nazmul . . . he . . . anything he say, then whoooshhh (*noise of fast movement*).

page 2

page 1

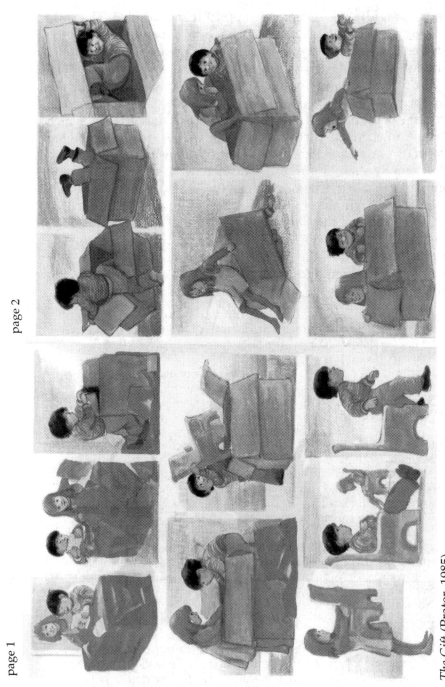

The Gift (Prater, 1985)
Reprinted from J. Prater (1985) *The Gift*, by permission of Bodley Head and Viking Penguin Inc

The Gift (Prater, 1985)
Reprinted from J. Prater (1985) *The Gift*, by permission of Bodley Head and Viking Penguin Inc

The telling continues to the end of the book. What this written transcript does not reflect is the excitement and involvement of the two children. With his very limited range of English words Nazmul is able to communicate well his understanding of the text. On several occasions he demonstrates that he is paying attention to the detail in the pictures. There are sections in the whole transcript when Nazmul does not have the English vocabulary to relate the events but then he uses sound effects to communicate the meaning and create the atmosphere. Syriah, telling the story in her community language, tells with the same excitement and expression and Nazmul can, of course, understand her contributions, which he builds on. Both children are clearly involved in the book and gaining a great deal of satisfaction from the experience. The teacher has provided some of the relevant vocabulary through her initial telling of the story and Nazmul draws on this demonstration in his version. Their experiences of interactions with picture books, such as this one, serve to reinforce the pleasures of reading, as well as allowing them to draw on existing skills of storytelling in their community language. Such books also teach the necessary knowledge about story structure and even characterisation.

Once beginner readers move into picture books with text, it is important to ensure that the books they are offered are supportive in many ways. We need to consider whether the content of the book presupposes a familiarity with particular aspects of British culture. Delightful and innovative as they are, books like Janet and Allan Ahlberg's *Each Peach, Pear, Plum* (1978) or *The Jolly Postman* (1986), with their intertextual references to English nursery rhymes and traditional stories, would not be appreciated by children who are unfamiliar with these. There are many picture books which, though not so deeply embedded in the childhood culture of Britain, still contain references to a particular way of life. Look, for example, at *The Giant Jam Sandwich* (Lord and Burroway, 1972), which is set in an English village with thoroughly 'English' characters and assumes prior knowledge about jam sandwiches! This is not to suggest that such books should be avoided but that they should perhaps be included later, when those new to English and the British way of life have become more familiar with the new culture.

There is, however, a place for picture books which introduce aspects of British culture, the culture of the school and in particular the traditional story heritage. It is in the realm of daily life in Britain that author/illustrator Shirley Hughes has a great deal to offer. Her 'Alfie' stories deal with universals of family life in a closely observed setting of domestic detail. In *Alfie Gets in First* (1981), the story begins with mum and two small children returning from shopping: the baby in the buggy, the loaded shopping basket and familiar city streets, cats, dogs, neighbours, milkman and window cleaner are likely to be recognised by all children. In another Alfie story, *Alfie's Feet* (1982), Alfie stamps in puddles, gets his feet wet and is subsequently taken to a crowded shopping centre to buy Wellington boots so that he can splash in puddles and keep his feet dry. This too provides a context to which all children can relate. Shirley Hughes' illustration in these books, and indeed in all her work, is prolific in the detail of many aspects of domestic and community life and provides a rich source of information for children who are new to it. Janet and Allan Ahlberg's work also includes picture books which are informative about the paraphernalia of babies and domestic life (*The Baby's Catalogue*, 1984) and, most relevantly, about school. In *Starting School* (1988) the routines of the day in a realistic, multicultural classroom are presented in a lively, reassuring way. There are many exciting picture books which both reflect children's life experiences and provide support for early literacy; a wide range of these needs to be available.

Equally the many versions of traditional fairy stories should be a part of the classroom provision. This is not usually a problem in early years and Key Stage 1 classrooms (4–7-year-olds) but they are seen less frequently in Key Stage 2 (7–11-year-olds). It would be important to include them at this stage when there are older children, newly arrived in Britain. Versions of traditional stories from other cultures are often similar to the ones we know and if these are available (perhaps in languages in which children are already literate) it helps newcomers to draw parallels and make sense of the new versions they encounter (see, for example, *Chinye* – Onyefulu and Safarewicz, 1994). There is so much literature in English which presupposes a knowledge of traditional tales that they are a necessary part of the acculturation process.

Books which are set in other countries, whether these are places known to the children or not, widen all children's horizons and demonstrate, at the same time, that not all stories are set in England and that all peoples and places are of value. Few children in British schools, whatever their ethnic background, will have had first-hand experience of Kenya, but all will respond to the simple storyline and the vibrant illustration of *Handa's Surprise* (Browne, 1994) and to the repetitive, cumulative, traditional rhyming story *Bringing the Rain to Kapiti Plain* (Aardema and Vidal, 1981), with its illustrations reflecting the landscape and the heat. The series of books by Mwenye Hadithi and Adrienne Kennaway (*Greedy Zebra*, 1984; *Hot Hippo*, 1986; *Crafty Chameleon*, 1987; *Tricky Tortoise*, 1988; *Lazy Lion*, 1990; *Baby Baboon*, 1993; *Hungry Hyena*, 1994), also set in Kenya and the East African plains, are a wonderful resource for the slightly more fluent reader. The richly coloured illustration reflecting the heat of the landscape makes the African setting abundantly clear to the reader whilst introducing the wealth of wildlife to the reader.

It is harder to find picture story books for beginner readers featuring characters from a variety of ethnic backgrounds in a British setting. There is a growing number about children from African-Caribbean backgrounds – *My Brother Sean* (Petronella Breinburg & Errol Lloyd), *Ten, Nine, Eight* (Molly Bang), *Eat Up, Gemma* (Sarah Hayes and Jan Ormerod), *Grandfather and I* (Helen Buckley and Jan Ormerod), *Nini at Carnival* (Errol Lloyd), *So Much* (Trish Cooke and Helen Oxenbury) – but fewer featuring children from other backgrounds. *Jyoti's Journey* (Ganley, 1986) which is now over ten years old, is a significant book, using collage to reflect the differing atmospheres encountered by a small girl who moves from India to England. Bernard Ashley and Derek Brazell's *Cleversticks* (1992), set in a lively multicultural classroom, is about Ling Sung and the recognition of his skill in using chopsticks. *A Balloon for Grandad* (Gray and Ray, 1988) recognises the situation of many children who have family members in other countries, with a story of an escaped balloon which, the child is persuaded, floats off to his grandfather Abdulla on an island with date trees and goats. Another one is to be found unexpectedly in the 'Topsy and Tim' series by Jean and Gareth Adamson, *Topsy and Tim Meet New Friends* (1990), when the children meet a Sikh family and even learn some numbers in Panjabi, whilst Shirley Hughes' 'Trotter Street Tales' (1989a; 1989b; 1991), about children and adults from a variety of groups, reflect a lively and diverse community. Teachers need to be constantly on the look out for good picture books which reflect the diversity in our society, though wary of books written to a 'multiethnic' brief, which can often be tokenistic. This diversity is perhaps more fully represented in longer books and fiction for older readers.

Alongside these books we also need to include as wide a variety as possible of picture books with text in the languages known to the children. Even when children are not literate in another language, they are likely to have seen examples of writing in their community languages in homes and in the wider environment. Sometimes they will be familiar with other written scripts, which have different conventions from English. It is important to recognise this experience and to demonstrate that the school values the linguistic diversity which is part of the children's experience. For those who are able to read already in another language it is essential to make provision for them to continue to read in that language while they are becoming fluent in English. Many literacy skills will be transferable and will continue to be developed in the first languages. It is not always easy to locate picture books in all the languages represented in schools, and there continues to be discussion about whether we should be seeking 'dual-text' books or parallel versions of the same book, where the text is translated and published as a separate book. The Multilingual Resources for Children Project, *Building Bridges* (1995), includes a very interesting discussion of many of these issues. Some dual-text books have been produced where the minority language was apparently given lower status than English, but there are now many high-quality ones where this is not so. Some books, recently published by Mantra, show clearly what is possible. *All the Colours of the Earth* (Hamanaka, 1996) has a lyrical text and richly coloured illustration and is available in a range of languages, with English. Another of the titles is *Savitri: A Tale of Ancient India* (Shepard and Rosenberry, 1997), which tells the traditional story from the *Mahabharata*, with delicate illustration perfectly matched to the Indian setting. This is available in all the Indian languages, with English.

સમય જતાં સત્યવાન રાજા બન્યો, અને સાવિત્રી બની તેની રાણી. પ્રભુની કૃપાથી તેમને
ઘણાં સંતાન થયાં, અને બન્નેએ લાંબુ અને સુખી જીવન ગાળ્યું. આથી જ્યારે યમરાજા તેમને
મૃત્યુલોકમાં લઇ જવા ફરી પાછા આવ્યા ત્યારે તેમને નહોતો કોઇ ડર કે ન હતાં કોઇ આંસુ.

In time, Satyavan became king and Savitri his queen. They lived long and happily,
blessed with many children. So they had no fears or tears when Yama came once again
to carry them to his kingdom.

Savitri: A Tale of Ancient India (Shepard and Rosenberry, 1997)

Hard-back picture books of this quality can be enjoyed by
children's families in their community/heritage language and,
even if family members do not read English, the story can be
talked about when it is shared at home. The same thing can
happen when children have parallel versions of a picture book
available in heritage languages. Some of the most popular picture books for beginner readers are produced in a range of
languages, some as dual language texts, some as parallel texts –
for example, Eric Carle's *The Very Hungry Caterpillar* (1970),
Eric Hill's *Spot* books (1980), Waddell and Firth's *Can't you
Sleep, Little Bear?* (1988) and Waddell and Benson's *Owl Babies*
(1992).

One of the most important contributions made by picture
books to developing knowledge of English, as well as literacy
skills, is the real linguistic support they give to those new to

English and new to literacy. Here we should be seeking books with settings all children will recognise, with language which is memorable and which uses the real linguistic structures of English rather than controlled vocabulary (whether that be 'key words' or phonically regular words) which can often be stilted and artificial. With text like 'My cat likes to hide in boxes. The cat from France, liked to sing and dance. But my cat likes to hide in boxes. The cat from Spain flew an aeroplane, the cat from France liked to sing and dance. But my cat likes to hide in boxes' (*My Cat Likes to Hide in Boxes*, Sutton and Dodd, 1973), the reader is presented with an entertaining, cumulative and predictable rhyming story. The repetition enables the child to join in very quickly, whilst the accompanying illustration supports prediction of the rhyming words. Michael Rosen and Helen Oxenbury's retelling of *We're Going on a Bear Hunt* (1989) is another example of a picture book with rhythmic, repetitive text and sound effects to describe the different kinds of movement. Here Helen Oxenbury's wonderful illustrations capture the movements, both fast and slow, the excitement and apprehension of the bear hunters, again providing visual support for the words of the text. Whilst the readers are enjoying the story, the text provides at the same time chunks of understandable language which have a natural structure: 'What a beautiful day.' 'We're not scared.' 'We can't go over it. We can't go under it. Oh no! We've got to go through it.' By the time the story has been read and reread several times, these structures will have become internalised. Jill Murphy's *Peace at Last* (1980) has the same memorable language structures. Mr Bear's 'Oh no! I can't stand this' became a much-used exclamation in one multilingual reception classroom whenever children were frustrated, bored or unwilling to tidy up! It was used equally accurately by children who were monolingual and children using English as an additional language. The language lessons provided by books like these are incidental in the process of learning to read, though there are other picture books which might be used to teach particular vocabulary.

Perhaps the best known of these is *Brown Bear, Brown Bear, What Do You See?* (Martin and Carle, 1984), which covers both colours and animal names in the context of a rhyming story. Here the illustration, in bold primary colours, provides all the clues to the text, whilst keeping a humorous touch with 'a blue horse' and 'a purple cat'. A more recent book, *Simpkin* (Blake, 1989), offers potential for explicit teaching of opposites – 'nasty, nice; fast, slow; high, low; up, down; weak, strong' – through rhyme, though it would be a pity if Quentin Blake's delightfully humorous text were to be seen as only having that purpose. The idiosyncrasies of the English spelling system can be observed and discussed through work on rhyming texts of all kinds and Quentin Blake has produced many of these: *Mister Magnolia* (1980), *ABC* (1989), *All Join In* (1990). *ABC* is a superb example of an alphabet book which is more than a boring list of words. Blake adds rhyming couplets to a set of detailed whole-page pictures, which are full of movement and detail; each picture is a story in itself! For children new to English, this book alone is a treasure trove of information and possibilities for discussion and explanation of words and ideas.

Indeed alphabet books, some of which are now very sophistic-ated, are an important source of information about the vocabul-ary and pronunciation of English. For very young children, pictures with simple naming text, for example Fiona Pragoff's *Alphabet* (1985), can develop confidence. Ruth Brown's *A Four-tongued Alphabet* (1991) offers single-word captions for framed paintings, in English, French, German and Spanish and could lead to some interesting discussion about the similarities be-tween the words in the four languages. For inner-city children, Rachel Isadora's evocative black-and-white drawings for *City Seen from A to Z* (1983), though set in New York, provide illustra-tions of a wider-ranging vocabulary. At the most sophisticated end of the scale there is *Animalia* (Base, 1986), full of brilliantly coloured, fantastic illustration, with almost limitless oppor-tunities for naming of objects and an ideal starting point for talking about alliteration. There are many kinds of beautifully illustrated alphabet books available, and in classrooms where there are children learning English, whether beginners or later-stage learners, these must be a central resource.

Using a range of picture books to support learners of English as an additional language requires the use of a range of teaching strategies. One of the most important will be the creation of many opportunities for children to hear stories and rhymes read aloud so that the tunes and patterns of English become more familiar. This will sometimes be a whole-class activity, when new books will be introduced and old favourites revisited, and sometimes a small group or individual activity; the books read will then need to be available to the children to practise new literacy skills in reading them to themselves and each other. Many of the favourites are available commercially as enlarged texts for shared reading, but where they are not it is worth producing 'big book' versions yourself. Shared reading provides an excellent teaching context; the teacher can focus on direct teaching about many aspects of English, ranging from verb endings, adjectives and prepositions to rhymes, alliteration and punctuation, in the context of stimulating picture book texts. Shared reading leads naturally into shared writing, the collaborative composition of new texts; writing with others provides a non-threatening and supportive context for using English with learners new to the language, throughout Key Stage 1 and Key Stage 2. The texts produced, when published as books in the classroom, also provide accessible, known texts for reading. There are case-study examples illustrating some of the range of possibilities in Barrs's (1990) *Shared Reading, Shared Writing* from the Centre for Language in Primary Education (CLPE). Two other books for teachers published by CLPE are a very useful source of information about texts and teaching approaches, *The Core Book. A Structured Approach to Using Books within the Reading Curriculum* (Ellis and Barrs, 1996) and the accompanying annotated booklist, *The Core Booklist* (Lazim and Moss, 1997). Though not specifically addressed to the needs of learners of English as an additional language (EAL), the teaching strategies and texts identified here would be immensely supportive to them.

There needs to be additional provision in classrooms where there are children new to English to enable understanding of the English encountered in the books to be reinforced and extended. Opportunities for dramatic play and drama related to the books allow the newly acquired language to be used and practised; this can include appropriate dressing-up clothes and masks, puppets and artifacts as well as story props and cut-outs. Equally, tape-recorded readings should be provided, together with copies of the books, so that they can be revisited again and again.

A picture book can often be a springboard into other curriculum areas and can introduce vocabulary relating to these areas in a supportive and comprehensible context. Consideration of distant places (geography) could begin with picture books like those set in Kenya (see above) and environmental issues through *Rainforest* (Cowcher, 1988), *Oi! Get off our Train* (Burningham, 1989), *Dear Greenpeace* (James, 1991) or *Brother Eagle, Sister Sky* (Chief Seattle and Jeffers, 1992). *Dear Greenpeace* also incidentally teaches the conventions of letter writing. The vocabulary needed to tell the time in English can be introduced through *What's the Time, Mr Wolf?* (Hawkins, 1994) and a range of mathematical concepts through *Maths Curse* (Scieszka and Smith, 1995). Encouragement to look closely at European fine art is provided by *I Spy: An Alphabet in Art* (1992) or *I Spy: Animals in Art* (1994), both by Lucy Micklethwait. There are many picture books which help to explain the notion of time passing and life in the past, starting with Martin Waddell and Penny Dale's *Once there were Giants* (1989) which follows one little girl from infancy to the time she has her own little girl and has illustrations which are full of visual references to her future and her past. Waddell and Johnson take the idea of family history for *Grandma's Bill* (1990) and Dupasquier and Bradman take a look across centuries in *The Sandal* (1989).

Many of the picture books referred to above are ones which are most suitable for older children. These are not simple books for the very young; though the actual text in many is very straightforward, the ideas, themes and topics are appropriate for older readers. The idea that 'picture books are for babies' – a comment often made by children in Key Stage 2 – is one which teachers will need to demonstrate is untrue. There are many picture books in which there are subjects to challenge older readers but with text which a beginner in English would be able to read; these are a valuable resource for the less fluent monolingual reader as well as for those with English as an additional language, for whom they should be available at the end of Key Stage 2 and beyond. Some authors and illustrators have created particularly appropriate books for this stage. Look, for example, at the often surreal work of Anthony Browne, the comic-strip formats of Phillipe Dupasquier, the jewel-like colours and environmental awareness in the work of Michael Foreman, the arresting pen-and-ink and colour-wash illustration of Charles Keeping, the complex and thought-provoking issues tackled by

Maurice Sendak, the unusual narrative structures used by John Burningham.

For all readers the contribution that picture books can make to the development of true literacy is enormous, as the range of topics covered in this book demonstrates. But for those of our pupils using English as an additional language, whether they are 4 or 14, a carefully chosen collection of picture books can provide the key to both the structures of the English language and the successful development of literacy in English. If children are given the chance to meet such books and teachers make use of the teaching opportunities they afford, much can be achieved, for the 'input' from them is utterly 'comprehensible' and the pleasure they give to children can remove much of the stress from having to get to grips with literacy in a new language.

Acknowledgement

My thanks to Anny Northcote of the former Unified Language Service support team in Tower Hamlets for the transcript of the reading of *The Gift*.

Bibliography

Aardema, V. and Vidal, B. (1981) *Bringing the Rain to Kapiti Plain*, Basingstoke: Macmillan.

Adamson, J. and Adamson, G. (1990) *Topsy and Tim Meet New Friends*, Glasgow: Blackie.

Ahlberg, J. and Ahlberg, A. (1978) *Each Peach, Pear, Plum*, Harmondsworth: Picture Puffin.

Ahlberg, J. and Ahlberg, A. (1986) *The Jolly Postman*, London: Viking Kestrel.

Ahlberg, J. and Ahlberg, A. (1988) *Starting School*, London: Viking Kestrel.

Ashley, B. and Brazell, D. (1992) *Cleversticks*, London: HarperCollins.

Bang, M. (1983) *Ten, Nine, Eight*, Harmondsworth: Picture Puffin.

Barrs, M. (ed.) (1990) *Shared Reading, Shared Writing* London: CLPE.

Base, G. (1986) *Animalia*, London: Viking Kestrel.

Blake, Q. (1980) *Mister Magnolia*, London: Jonathan Cape.

Blake, Q. (1989) *ABC*, London: Jonathan Cape.

Blake, Q. (1990) *All Join In*, London: Jonathan Cape.

Blake, Q. (1993) *Simpkin*, London: Jonathan Cape.

Bradman, T. and Dupasquier, P. (1989) *The Sandal*, Harmondsworth: Picture Puffin.

Breinburg, P and Lloyd, E. (1975) *My Brother Sean*, London: Red Fox.

Brown, R. (1991) *A Four-tongued Alphabet*, London: Andersen Press.

Browne, E. (1994) *Handa's Surprise*, London: Walker Books.

Buckley, H. and Ormerod, J. (1995) *Grandfather and I*, London: Viking.

Burningham, J. (1989) *Oi! Get off our Train*, London: Jonathan Cape.

Carle, E. (1970) *The Very Hungry Caterpillar*, London: Hamish Hamilton (dual-language editions published by Mantra).

Chief Seattle and Jeffers, S. (1992) *Brother Eagle, Sister Sky*, London: Hamish Hamilton.

Cooke, T. and Oxenbury, H. (1994) *So Much*, London: Walker Books.

Cowcher, H. (1988) *Rainforest*, London: André Deutsch.

Ellis, S. and Barrs, M. (eds.) (1996) *The Core Book. A Structured Approach to Using Books within the Reading Curriculum*, London: CLPE, use with accompanying booklist, *The Core Booklist*.

Ganley, H. (1986) *Jyoti's Journey*, London: André Deutsch.

Gray, N. and Ray, J. (1988) *A Balloon for Grandad*, London: Orchard.

Gregory, E. (1996) *Making Sense of a New World. Learning to Read in a Second Language*, London: Paul Chapman.

Hadithi, M. and Kennaway, A. (1984) *Greedy Zebra*, London: Hodder & Stoughton.

Hadithi, M. and Kennaway, A. (1986) *Hot Hippo*, London: Hodder & Stoughton.

Hadithi, M. and Kennaway, A. (1987) *Crafty Chameleon*, London: Hodder & Stoughton.

Hadithi, M. and Kennaway, A. (1988) *Tricky Tortoise*, London: Hodder & Stoughton.

Hadithi, M. and Kennaway, A. (1990) *Lazy Lion*, London: Hodder & Stoughton.

Hadithi, M. and Kennaway, A. (1993) *Baby Baboon*, London: Hodder & Stoughton.

Hadithi, M. and Kennaway, A. (1994) *Hungry Hyena*, London: Hodder & Stoughton.

Hamanaka, S. (1996) (Yoruba/English text) *All the Colours of the Earth*, London: Mantra.

Hawkins, C. (1994) *What's the Time, Mr Wolf?* London: Mammoth.

Hayes, S. and Ormerod, J. (1988) *Eat Up, Gemma*, London: Walker Books.

Hill, E. (1980) *Where's Spot?* London: Heinemann (available in many single-language editions; also dual-language editions from Roy Yates Books, Small Fields Cottage, Cox Green, Rudgwick, Horsham, West Sussex RH12 3DE.

Hughes, S. (1981) *Alfie Gets in First*, London: Bodley Head.

Hughes, S. (1982) *Alfie's Feet*, London: Bodley Head.

Hughes, S. (1989a) *The Big Concrete Lorry (A Tale of Trotter Street)*, London: Walker Books.

Hughes, S. (1989b) *Angel Mae (A Tale of Trotter Street)*, London: Walker Books.

Hughes, S. (1991) *Wheels (A Tale of Trotter Street)*, London: Walker Books.

Isadora, R. (1983) *City Seen from A to Z*, New York: Mulberry Books.

James, S. (1991) *Dear Greenpeace*, London: Walker Books.

Krashen, S. and Terrell, T. (1983) *The Natural Approach: Language Acquisition in the Classroom*, Oxford: Pergamon Press.

Lazim, A. and Moss, E. (1997 edition) *The Core Booklist*, London: CLPE.

Lloyd, E. (1978) *Nini at Carnival*, Harmondsworth: Picture Puffin.

Lord, J.V. and Burroway, J. (1972) *The Giant Jam Sandwich* , London: Jonathan Cape.

Martin, B. Jr and Carle, E. (1984) *Brown Bear, Brown Bear, What Do You See?* London: Hamish Hamilton.

Micklethwait, L. (1992) *I Spy: An Alphabet in Art*, London: HarperCollins.

Micklethwait, L. (1994) *I Spy: Animals in Art*, London: HarperCollins.

Murphy, J. (1980) *Peace At Last*, London: Macmillan.
Onyefulu, O. and Safarewicz, E. (1994) *Chinye*, London: Frances Lincoln.
Pragoff, F. (1985) *Alphabet*, London: Victor Gollancz.
Prater, J. (1985) *The Gift*, London: Bodley Head.
Rosen, M. and Oxenbury, H. (1989) *We're Going on a Bear Hunt*, London: Walker Books.
Scieszka, J. and Smith, L. (1995) *Maths Curse*, London: Viking.
Shepard, A. and Rosenberry, V. (1997) (Panjabi/English text) *Savitri: A Tale of Ancient India*, London: Mantra.
Sutton, E. and Dodd, L. (1973) *My Cat Likes to Hide in Boxes*, London: Hamish Hamilton.
Waddell, M. and Benson, P. (1992) *Owl Babies*, London: Walker Books (this title and *Can't you Sleep, Little Bear?* are available in dual-language editions, published by Magi Books, Hayes).
Waddell, M. and Dale, P. (1989) *Once there were Giants*, London: Walker Books.
Waddell, M. and Firth, B. (1988) *Can't you Sleep, Little Bear?* London: Walker Books.
Waddell, M. and Johnson, J. (1990) *Grandma's Bill*, London: Simon & Schuster.

Chapter 6

'Real boys don't go to dance classes': challenging gender stereotypes

Janet Evans

'What are you doing, Steven?' asked his mother.
'I'm pliéing like Theresa does in dance classes.'
'You don't want to do that,' she said. Steven was puzzled. I do, he thought.
'Mum, can I go to dance classes?' His mother's mouth opened wide.
'Certainly not. Real boys don't go to dance classes.'
(Ormerod and Magorian, Jump, 1992)

Even after just four pages of *Jump* where the above dialogue takes place, it is more than obvious that the boy in this story is very much a *real* boy. Magorian tells of Steven, a small boy who is obliged to watch his sister participating in the physically demanding world of ballet – with, he is quick to note, some boys. He is perplexed to find that when he wants to join in his mum tells him that dance classes are not for real boys. Through a series of events his problem is eventually resolved and his mother realises that not only will he eventually make a fine basketball player but he will also make a fine dancer too despite the fact that he is a boy.

The text, already full of description, movement and emotion is really enhanced by Jan Ormerod's illustrations. She portrays Steven as a lively, alert child who is keen on action but also as a sensitive child who is not going to be influenced by sentiments which he feels don't apply to him. Steven is more than capable of being persistent in order to get what he wants. Ormerod

At the next class, when the boys were jumping, Steven couldn't sit still any longer.

He ran across the floor.

His father tried to pull him away.

"Let him stay," said the teacher.

"He's good."

After the jumps the teacher said, "Show me what else you can do, Steven."

So he did.

The children clapped.

"Would you like to be in the show this year?" the teacher asked.

"Will you teach me a basketball dance?" asked Steven.

The teacher laughed.

"Well," she said, "I'll see."

Jump (Ormerod and Magorian, 1992)
Illustrations © Jan Ormerod, written by Michelle Magorian (1992). Reprinted by permission of the publisher, Walker Books Ltd, London

cleverly uses three double-page spreads to share with the reader the notion of boys in action: in the first, big boys are shown playing basketball on television, then Steven himself is shown full of anger in his bedroom this leads on to a third, wonderfully vital page where Steven is to be seen physically moving across the page in a series of fairly action-packed karate-type movements. The message from this book, a wonderful alliance of word and pictures, is clear and unequivocable: boys can and do dance as well as girls and they can do it very well.

Much has been written over the last two decades about the way in which children's literature has portrayed women and men, girls and boys in specific, gender stereotyped roles. Steven's initial situation in *Jump* makes us mindful of other books and indeed real-life situations which don't allow for flexibility in relation to gender stereotypes: books in which it is accepted without question that girls do *not* play football, rugby or cricket and boys do *not* play with dolls, play houses or feed the baby. Many of these gender stereotypes are slowly but surely being challenged and replaced by more egalitarian thoughts; however, negative stereotypes still linger in some people's minds.

Research looking at gender bias in children's books (Freebody and Baker, 1987), including reading schemes and picture books, found that the roles played by both male and female characters frequently conformed to traditional, stereotyped images, with women in submissive, 'in-the-home' type roles and men involved in more active, outdoor activities. These gender stereotyped images were created by both the text and the illustrations working together. Often, however, the illustrations alone portrayed men and boys in stereotyped male activities, e.g. cleaning cars, going out to work as the main 'bread winner', climbing trees and being in adventures, whilst women and girls were left in stereotyped female activities, e.g. doing the housework, baking and looking after babies or looking frightened as they wait to be rescued from danger. Some of the more recent reading schemes show improvements on this situation and many picture book authors and illustrators such as Jan Ormerod, Mary Hoffman, Eileen Browne and others are increasingly much more aware of the need to present images of boys and girls in non-stereotyped situations. Babette Cole, for example, presents beautifully outlandish and funny non-stereotyped images of adult men and women with boys and girls as the voice of reason.

Recent research into the role that children's literature has to play in channelling children along particular gendered paths has resulted in some interesting information. Gilbert (1994) looked at why, when it is obvious that girls have ability and opportunity and often perform better in exams than boys, many girls leave school with modest ambitions. Gilbert surmised that something happens to girls which leaves them with the impression that they are not as good as, are less talented than and cannot do as well as the men who surround them in later life, e.g. husbands and bosses. She states that it is the texts that surround us in our culture that tell us how to 'read' the world. These texts tell us what it is to be a man or a woman in today's society, that is, we are 'positioned' by the texts and hence begin to act accordingly. The texts go further and tell other people how to view us; hence, woman are expected to act as women and men as men.|Concepts of femininity and masculinity are constantly and continually being constructed by media texts, including television, journals, newspapers and advertisements. Women are seen as passive, childrearing dishwashers who have soft hands, whilst men are active, professional smoothies who race about in flash cars looking cool and handsome.

When we begin to look at texts for young children we can see many examples of these 'gendered discourses': nursery rhymes, songs, children's television and, of course, books all provide ample examples of gendered roles. It would seem then that the simple act of ensuring that children have access to literature in which both girls and boys are seen as equals, doing similar activities, might actually change people's stereotypes. However, Davies and Banks (1992) found that even when children were presented with non-gender stereotyped literature which depicted girls and boys as equals, they still kept to their existing viewpoints which had already been shaped by previous exposure to gender discourses which in themselves are reflections of the dominant discourse of Western culture and society. Davies and Banks assert that unless children are given the opportunity to talk about and begin to understand how the gendered discourse works then no amount of exposure to literature claiming that girls and boys are equal will change their views.

The opportunity to respond to texts and to begin to deconstruct the meaning of texts is therefore a crucial step along the road to allowing children to become aware of how they can be positioned by texts.

Millard (1997) – taking a different stance in looking at why boys are not achieving as well as girls in the humanities – felt that one reason was because they were being exposed to too much fiction delivered by women English teachers at both the primary and secondary level. Millard also found, in agreement with Davies and Banks (1992), that the role models in the home environment affected children's reading practices. Boys and girls were seeing their mums reading mainly fiction whilst dads were seen reading newspapers, information books and other non-fiction materials. A lot of the reading that children are expected to do at school is fiction; hence as Millard (1997, p. 13) states, 'Boys therefore, experienced a dissonance between the literacy they practised skilfully at home and that demanded from them by teachers'. Millard comments on the research which feminists have done in relation to providing non-gender stereotyped literature to encourage girls to develop better self-concepts. She contends (*ibid.*, p. 18) that 'this concern has created a lack of equity in a focus that considers the performance and interests of only one sex'. Millard accepts that gender is a socially constructed concept and she also acknowledges that 'English-speaking countries represent reading as an activity preferred by girls' (*ibid.*, p. 19). If, as has already been noted, reading is a social construct and girls and reading are often associated with each other, then Millard has a valid point in suggesting that boys are differently literate due to the dictates of their society and culture.

Daniels (1994), researching into the role that popular fiction (comics and magazines) plays in helping girls to adjust to and cope with everyday life, found that girls are not too worried at being seen doing 'boy-type' activities. Hence a girl would quite happily be seen carrying a copy of *Beano* out of a newsagent whilst a boy would 'not be seen dead' with a copy of *Bunty* or *Judy*. Millard (1994, p. 102) agrees with this analysis and comments on the fact that 'Dressing up in "male attire", acquiring boys' toys, and "trying on" a male role is part of most girls' early experience . . . The female role on the other hand is always an area that acts as transgressive for boys, an area of disquiet or ridicule'. Gilbert and Rowe (1989) in some earlier research found that whilst girls would read about boys and their activities, boys would not read about girls and their activities.

The whole picture is complex and has led to a great number of picture books published in the last few years striving to be politically correct with illustrations which try to portray human beings engaged in meaningful activities in appropriate situations. In a move which is a touch ironic and in many cases satirical, some picture books seem to have taken a sideways dig at the whole issue of gender stereotyping. The result has been a whole 'glut' of exquisitely humorous books where both text and accompanying illustrations address the issue of gender in an 'alternative' manner to that which has been previously tried. Books in this category include Anthony Browne's *Piggybook* (1986), *The Tough Princess* (1986) by Martin Waddell, *Princess Smartypants* (1986) and *Prince Cinders* (1987) by Babette Cole and, of course, Robert Munsch's *The Paper Bag Princess* (1980). There are many other books which may not be quite as mocking but which are still remarkably effective at challenging gender stereotypes, for example Hoffman and Burrough's *My Grandma Has Black Hair* (1988) and Hoffman's *Amazing Grace* (1991).

In an attempt to find out how children would respond to a well-known picture book which presents an alternative view of a traditional fairy story I decided to work with a class of thirty-six, 8 and 9-year-old children. Freemantle (1993), in her study of children's responses to fairy tales, felt that the fairy-tale genre allows young readers to deal with deeper issues, values and emotions in a more acceptable manner. She writes (*ibid.*, p. 64): 'children have an innate need to engage with the tangible, and the fairy-tale can act as an accessible metaphor for things not yet intellectually understood.' She also felt that traditional fairy stories often present the young reader with the opportunity to identify with characters who do brave and courageous deeds in dangerous situations against all odds or who look beautiful and wait to be rescued, thus reinforcing the notion that 'the reading materials children first encounter at school represent more than a vehicle for learning literacy skills, . . . the content of the materials speaks to children about growing up female or male.' (Gilbert and Rowe, 1989).

The Paper Bag Princess by Robert Munsch tells of Elizabeth, a beautiful princess who was going to marry a prince called Ronald. Ronald is seized and carried away by a dragon who also smashes her castle and burns her clothes. Elizabeth resorts to wearing a paper bag, the only thing she can find and sets about getting the prince back. In a series of clever, non-violent moves she totally exhausts the dragon and rescues Prince Ronald, who instead of gratefully accepting his deliverance from the claws of the dragon, starts to criticise Elizabeth for her tatty, non-princess like appearance. Elizabeth immediately tells Ronald what to do with himself and the intended wedding is cancelled. The last picture shows the back of Elizabeth gleefully skipping into the sunset as she celebrates a very lucky escape from a wimpish yet arrogant male chauvinist.

In this atypical fairy story Munsch as author and Martchenko as illustrator show no regard for the normally accepted, stereo-typed way in which prince, princess and dragon stories have historically evolved. They assume that their audience will be familiar with the traditional fairy-tale genre and that they will be able to use their familiarity to make sense of a text which challenges the norm. Although the characters, the beginning and the setting are kept almost the same as in most traditional fairy tales, the author brings about a totally different, unexpected resolution through subtly changing the plot. I felt *The Paper Bag Princess* was an ideal book to use to explore whether the children

1) had preconceived, gender stereotyped ideas of how traditional prince/princess fairy stories are constructed in terms of beginning, setting, characterisation, plot and resolution and whether their previous experiences with this genre affected the way they would respond to the book prior to the initial reading;
2) had previously formed ideas of what princes and princesses looked like and whether these images came from exposure to images in other books of the fairy-tale genre, for example, beautiful, helpless princesses with long hair and blue eyes and handsome princes who are tall, dark and protective;
3) thought the protagonist would be a male or a female and whom they thought would defeat the dragon;
4) were surprised by any aspects of the story when it was eventually read to them; and

5) would recognise that it was a parody on the traditional prince, princess and dragon fairy story.

Before reading the book the children were told that there were three story characters: a prince, a princess and a dragon who was eventually defeated. They were asked to give their ideas of what the story would be about. Their responses were quite surprising. Only one or two children told the story in a conventional way whereby the prince kills the dragon, saves the princess and they get married and live happily ever after. Jacqueline's response was of this type: 'The dragon took the princess to the cave, the prince came to the cave and killed the dragon, he cut him up and the princess came out. The prince and the princess lived happily ever after.'

The majority of the responses, however, had a rather unexpected twist. Faine's uncomplicated version was short and yet explicit: 'The story will be about a horrible prince and a nice princess. The dragon saves the princess from the prince!' Jenny's version was also short but had a surreal aspect to it in the form of a dragon with a hosepipe: 'The nasty prince burnt down the princess's house and the dragon came to save her. The fire fighter dragon had a hose pipe and squirted water and saved the princess!'

In the short period of time given to thinking about the storyline, Pascale showed a remarkable ability to express some quite complex thoughts:

> The nasty prince lived far away and wanted to kill the princess. The dragon heard about it because he read newspapers, he came out of his cave and found the prince . . . he saw him riding across the desert. The magic dragon turned himself small, then grew tall just as the prince got to the castle. He breathed fire and killed him . . . he died after he killed the prince.

In these unorthodox versions of the story it was the prince who was the 'baddy' and the dragon who saved the princess. However it was interesting to see that although the overall storyline might not be exactly as was expected, the princess was still perceived as the character who was weak and who needed saving from evil. As Gemma's response showed: 'The princess would be saved. It wouldn't be the dragon and the prince was too ugly to be saved.'

Having thought about the overall storyline and still prior to reading the book, each child was given one of three tasks. One task was to draw a picture and write a short description of the character who defeated the dragon to include how this character felt. Another task was to draw and write about the character who was saved, commenting on how this character felt. The third task was to draw the last picture in the book and write about the end of the story. The children's responses to these more specific tasks were surprising once again because far from supporting their initial, non-gender stereotyped ideas about what the overall story would be about, their character descriptions began to conform much more to the expected norm of fairy-story characters. All the children's responses were similar in their acceptance of gender roles, that is, the male prince was active and did the fighting and the female princess was passive, being gratefully appreciative of her brave prince.

The character who defeated the dragon

The boys were more overt in their references to princesses as weak creatures who constantly needed rescuing:

> James: The prince was tough and he might have weapons and princesses are weak.
> Peter: It couldn't be the princess because princesses don't always have weapons.
> Matthew: The prince might be tough, tougher than the princess and he might be the princess's boyfriend.
> James: Princesses are not into war 'n things, they always scream and run off. The dragon might chase after the princess.
> Matthew: The princess might run off and the prince will stay and fight.

The girls seemed almost programmed to accept the notion that princes are strong and brave. Several of them touched on concepts of goodness and badness and suitable justice being seen to be done, e.g. the naughty person is defeated:

> Sarah: The prince always defeats the naughty person because he is the bravest.
> Lauren: You never know, the princess might be strong and brave. The dragon is usually fierce.
> Hannah: In every story that I have read the prince kills the naughty person.
> Zoe: The princess is always beautiful with servants and the prince fights for her so that she won't get hurt.

Sarah's stereotyped portrayal of the character who defeated the dragon: the prince with his blood-thirsty killing instruments in his hands

The Prinse

I thinck that the prt prise is a good fiter, drave and angrey, and I thinck that the prise is going to de tolrl and have to wepns they are are an axs and a soud. He mit have a helmit wihb a Gether on it, and a bage, oG the casle. The prinse was a bit scerd. He is very hansome blowck

I think that the prince is a good fighter, brave and angry, and I think that the prince is going to be tall and have two weapons, they are an axe and a sword. He might have a helmet with a feather on it, and a badge of the castle. The prince was a bit scared. He is a very handsome bloke.

The character who was saved

The responses of both girls and boys conformed to stereotyped gender roles. Here, however, the influence of previously read literature and television programmes was more evident. The children were drawing on their knowledge of the way traditional stories are portrayed in traditional children's literature and by the media:

> Claire: The princess would be saved because in stories the prince usually saves the princess.
> Kate: Normally the princess would be saved because in stories the dragon captures the princess and the prince has to save her.

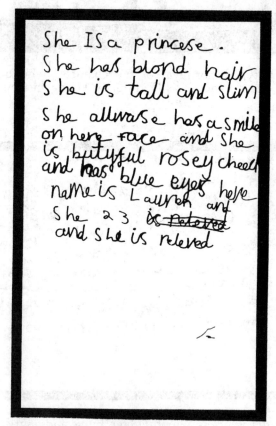

Lucy is a princess. She has blond hair. She is tall and slim. She always has a smile on her face and she has beautiful rosy cheeks and she has blue eyes. Her name is Lauren and she is 23 and she is relieved (*to have been rescued*).

Jonathan: The prince wouldn't have been captured because he would have a sword and he can fight a dragon. The princess would need to be rescued.

Steven: I've drawn a princess. No other character would be rescued because girls are weak.

Philip: On television programmes the prince usually gets slaughtered by the dragon.

The end of the story

Many of the children who considered how the story would end presented gender stereotyped resolutions:

Jonathan's stereotypical drawing of the character who was saved: the princess.

Anthony: The dragon should be dead, he was beating up the princess and she nearly died so the dragon should die. The prince kills it and the prince and princess live happily ever after.
Katie: The prince kills the dragon for bullying the princess. The dragon dies. The prince and princess go to live together in a new castle.
Elizabeth: The princess is captured by the dragon. The prince likes the princess and sets off to save her. The prince finds the dragon's cave and kills the dragon.

There were a few non-stereotyped resolutions and Simon presented a slightly different resolution which doesn't indicate who did the capturing: 'The dragon is captured and locked up, the Prince makes friends with him and feeds him and looks after him like a pet. The dragon could help with cooking because of his fiery breath.' Graham too had a different notion of how the story would end: 'After a battle they make friends because the dragon gives up.'

Elizabeth's contemporary portrayal of a very down-to-earth prince and princess standing alongside a bloody, sword-pierced dragon, somehow belies the obviously strong gender stereotyped undertones to her understanding of the text

> The prince rescued the princess from the dragon
> He felt very proud of what he had done So did
> his father the princesses father was more
> than pleased he was delitghted. The prince
> feeling very bold and brave. Went out and
> the dragon came out of his cave. and the
> prince Ikilled him by sticking his sword into the
> dragon. the dragon was defeated for ever.
> THE END

(Elizabeth's very neat solution to the story (prereading) shows a strong awareness of the fairy-story genre with all the associated gender stereotyping of character roles): The prince rescued the princess from the dragon. He felt very proud of what he had done so did his father. The princess's father was more than pleased, he was delighted. The prince, feeling very bold and brave, went out and the dragon came out of his cave and the prince killed him by sticking his sword into the dragon. The dragon was defeated for ever. The end.

After the children had completed their particular task I read the book to them along with showing them the illustrations. The shared reading was accompanied by 'oohs' and 'aahs' and many exclamations of the 'I didn't think that would happen' type. The children were given the opportunity to respond to the text in small discussion groups and were then asked to write down some of the things that surprised them about the story. Their responses were quite revealing. It was evident that many of the children had expected the story to run along traditional gender stereotyped lines and were quite indignant when this story went 'against the grain'. They had a kind of 'how dare this story not do as it should' attitude. However their responses also disclosed the fact that far from being concerned about who did or didn't get rescued, killed or married, quite a few of the children were much more preoccupied with other, more unexpected details such as the fact that the paper bag didn't get burnt, even when faced with extreme heat. Incidentally none of the children questioned why the princess herself didn't get burnt . . . presumably it was taken for granted that the main good characters in a story do not die:

Steven: One of the things that surprised me in the story was that the prince got carried away. It surprised me because in all the other fairy stories the princess always gets carried away by the dragon. It surprised me that the princess wanted to save the prince. It surprised me because in a story the prince always saves the princess.

Jonathan: One of the things that surprised me was when the princess saved the prince and he shouted at the princess because she stunk and she was wearing a paper bag. And I thought that the princess would be captured and the prince would save the princess but it was the other way round.

Pascale: It surprised me because it is usually the princess who is captured. It surprised me when the princess called Ronald a toad. It just shows you that girls can do the same as boys. Girls are as brave and as strong as boys. And it surprised me that Ronald and Elizabeth said together 'We are NOT getting married, because you, Elizabeth, are not acting like a princess. You, Ronald are a wimp because you are scared'. It was surprising because usually they get married (*in these kinds of stories*).

Simon: One of the things that surprised me in the story was the clothes were burning but the paper bag wasn't. It surprised me because the paper bag wasn't burnt but the clothes were. The paper bag will burn easy but the clothes won't.

Zoe: One of the things that surprised me in the story was that the paper bag was not burnt, it surprised me because paper bags normally burn. Another thing that surprised me was that the dragon carried the prince off and it is normally the princess that gets carried off. Also another thing that surprised me was that the princess shouted at the dragon and she wasn't scared because in other films the princess is scared.

Gemma: One of the things that surprised me was the Paper Bag Princess went to the dragon's house to save Ronald. It surprised me because she would probably be scared if she was me. Another thing that surprised me was the dragon taking the prince away. It surprised me because it is usually the princess. Another thing that surprised me was the dragon flying round the world in ten seconds. It surprised me because nobody can fly that fast. Another thing that surprised me was them not getting married. It surprised me because they used to love each other.

Ben was a child who was more interested in how many forests the dragon burnt rather than with the sex of the protagonist or the paper bag not being burnt. His comment indicated that he was very much aware of how the fairy-tale genre usually ends: 'One of the things that surprised me in the story was that the dragon blew 50 forests and then 100. It surprised me because no other dragon has never done that in any other story.'

Some of the other readers were surprised to find that the protagonist was a girl and not a boy. They related what they heard in the story to their previous experiences with this genre. Elizabeth's response was a very clear example of this:

> One of the things that surprised me was that the dragon carried the prince off. It surprised me because in most fairy stories it is the princess that gets carried off. One of the other things that surprised me was that the princess didn't go away (*from the entrance to the cave*) but knocked again when the dragon stuck his head out. It surprised me because girls are weak usually in fairy stories.

Pidgeon (1993), in considering the links between learning reading and learning gender, points out that children's awareness of gender seems to follow the same kind of developmental pattern as cognitive development. She states (*ibid.*, p. 24) that 'learning about gender . . . will follow the same developmental pattern as other concepts, from concrete to abstract'. The concept of gender becomes an important issue for children between the ages of 3 and 7 and because gender is a complex concept, young children initially focus on the most obvious and most stereotypical differences and exhibit behaviour which links them with their gender. However, 'once the concept of permanent gender identity is established (around age ten) they no longer see sex-role differences as absolute, but as more of social convention that can be changed' (*ibid.*, p. 25).

When researchers first started looking at children's texts for gender stereotyping it was to show that it existed. There was a naive assumption that finding the evidence of stereotyping would be enough to persuade publishers, writers and illustrators not to produce books which encouraged traditional gender stereotyped views of men and women. This in turn would lead to the 'New Reader'. The New Reader, like the New Man, would only be presented with texts that had been through a politically correct seive. As a result the next generation would be free of stereotypes.

As we now know, this did not happen. Simply ridding books of gender stereotyping did not rid the world of stereotypes. Educators who were committed to teaching equity issues realised that some form of direct teaching was needed. In the first place this was done to get children to notice the different gender images and it involved engaging pupils in discourse about the role models presented in picture books. Several books, including *The Paper Bag Princess*, were used because they presented wonderful opportunities to discuss a particular genre, the fairy tale, and also because they promoted equal opportunities (Hughes, 1991). However the work carried out with this group of children shows yet again that such simplistic solutions need to be treated with care. Children may be able to complete tasks which force them to relate to non-traditional storylines in texts. However, they may not fully internalise the non-gender stereotypes being presented to them. If the concepts presented by the texts have not been fully understood then there will be no transfer of learning to real life. Hence, the children's fundamental thinking will not be changed by reading the literature.

The idea that children, or indeed adults, may be left unchanged by what they read is disquieting. Certainly the responses these children made gave us a window into the complex thoughts of the 8 and 9-year-old. Our own thoughts are often confused and intricate, so why should we be surprised to find that children's thoughts are equally as complex? The responses from this piece of work highlight a couple of other issues. First, children need to have a basic understanding and familiarity with the genre being examined in order to recognise when the traditional format has been deliberately changed. It was clear that some children lacked an awareness of the way fairy tales 'work'. Due to this lack of awareness they missed the humour of Robert Munsch's spoof and were left coping with a text that they did not understand. Secondly, some children had their own agendas. 'Why didn't the paper bag burn?' was an interesting question but not one which was being considered. The issue of gender stereotyping was at the top of the agenda for the teacher, yet for the child who posed this question, it was paper bags that didn't burn that were a top priority.

It is evident that authors of children's books and educators of young children cannot assume that children will automatically focus on what they expect them to focus on. Children respond to texts in diverse and sometimes unusual ways which draw on their previous experiences and which show their ability to make sense of texts according to what is meaningful for them at any given period in time. In using *The Paper Bag Princess* I tried to explore a few issues relating to gender stereotyping and in so doing I finished up with more questions than answers. The more opportunities we give children to read and interact with picture books, the better. However, the idea of challenging gender stereo-types through the use of picture books is not always as straight-forward as it seems. Even if children are allowed to discuss non-gender stereotyped books and are encouraged to deconstruct the 'hidden message' to facilitate better understanding of the wider issues at play, one still cannot guarantee that they will be fully aware of the potential or otherwise of their position as a male or female in their culture. Pidgeon (1993, p. 34) states: 'Reading may be one of the behaviours that reflects and confirms gender iden-tity, but it also has the potential to extend it.' The debate will obviously rage on but one of my solutions will be to keep reading!

Acknowledgements

Thanks go to Pat Hughes and Sue Pidgeon for their extremely helpful comments on this piece of work.

Bibliography

Browne, A. (1986) *Piggybook*, London: Julia MacRae.
Cole, B. (1986) *Princess Smartypants*, London: Picture Lions.
Cole, B. (1987) *Prince Cinders*, London: Picture Lions.
Daniels, J. (1994) 'Girl talk': the possibilities of popular fiction. In Styles, M., Bearne, E. and Watson, V. (eds.) *The Prose and the Passion: Children and the Their Reading*, London: Cassell.
Davies, B. and Banks, C. (1992) The gender trap: a feminist poststructuralist anal-ysis of primary school children's talk about gender. In Holland, J. and Blair, M. with Sheldon, S. (1995) *Debates and Issues in Feminist Research and Pedagogy*, Clevedon: Multilingual Matters in association with the Open University.
Freebody, P. and Baker, C. (1987) Children's first schoolbooks: introductions to the culture of literacy. In Pauwels, A. (ed.) *Women and Language in Australian and New Zealand Society*, Sydney: Australian Professional Publications.
Freemantle, S. (1993) 'Once upon a time' – a study of children's responses to fairytale. In Pinsent, P. (ed.) *The Power of the Page: Children's Books and their Readers*, London: David Fulton Publishers in association with the Roehampton Institute.

Gilbert, P. (1994) *Divided by a Common Curriculum? Gender and the English Curriculum*, Melbourne, Vic.: Curriculum Corporation.

Gilbert, P. with Rowe, K. (1989) *Gender, Literacy and the Classroom*, Victoria: Australian Reading Association.

Hoffman, M. (1991) *Amazing Grace*, London: Frances Lincoln.

Hoffman, M. and Burroughs, J. (1988) *My Grandma Has Black Hair*, London: Beaver Books.

Hughes, P. (1991) *Gender Issues and the Primary Classroom*, London: Scholastic.

Millard, E. (1994) *Developing Readers in the Middle Years*, Buckingham: Open University Press.

Millard, E. (1997) *Differently Literate: Boys, Girls and the Schooling of Literacy*, London: Falmer Press.

Munsch, R. (1980) *The Paper Bag Princess*, London: Hippo Books.

Ormerod, J. and Magorian, M. (1992) *Jump*, London: Walker Books.

Pidgeon, S. (1993) Learning reading and learning gender. In Barrs, M. and Pidgeon, S. (eds.) *Reading the Difference*, London: Centre for Language in Primary Education.

Waddell, M. (1986) *The Tough Princess*, London: Walker Books.

Chapter 7

Exploring visual literacy across the curriculum

Pat Hughes

What is visual literacy?

We live in bright colourful worlds where we are surrounded by visual images which move and change size, shape, depth and colour before our very eyes. As educators, one of our primary purposes is to help children make sense of this world, even when it seems to compete with formal schooling. Media education examines ways in which visual images are used, but the concept of 'visual literacy' is much wider than this. The model (see Figure 7.1) shows different aspects of visual literacy with which learners need to become familiar and confident. Some aspects are life long, such as reading images in the world around us; others, such as reading the pictures to inform the text, may be just starting points in learning another skill. Several chapters in this book look at ways in which picture books – both the text and the picture – can be used to promote literacy. This chapter looks at picture books from another perspective. The first section explores some of the ways in which picture books support visual literacy, while the second part provides some examples of how fictional picture books can be used to develop children's learning of subject knowledge through their skills of visual literacy.

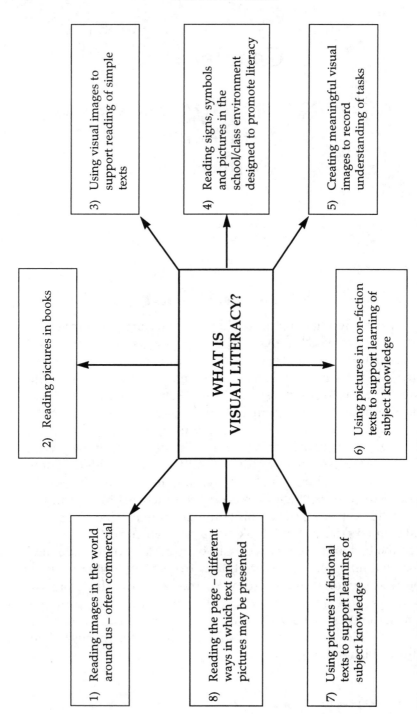

Figure 7.1   Visual literacy across the curriculum

Using picture books to support visual literacy

Learning to read pictures

The ability to 'read pictures' is vital and the term visual literacy can be used to describe a crosscurricular skill, like numeracy, IT and literacy, which children need to use in every area of the curriculum. It is also a life skill and much of the material on visual literacy in primary schools (Maidenhead Teachers' Centre, 1988; DEC, 1989; Hampshire LEA, 1989) acknowledges this and looks at ways in which children's out-of-school experiences can be used to enhance their visual literacy in school. Despite literature such as the publications mentioned above, it is often a crosscurricular skill which is taken for granted. One of the few government statements about crosscurricular skills in the English National Curriculum (NCC, 1989) only identifies oracy, literacy, numeracy, graphicacy and problem-solving as cross-curricular skills to be developed through all subjects. Nor is teaching visual literacy recognised as a required standard for intending teachers. The criteria set out for initial teacher training in England in 1997 require students to 'exploit, in all their teaching, opportunities to develop children's language, reading, numeracy, information handling and other skills'. The term visual literacy gets no mention either on its own merit or as part of the whole curriculum.

Learning to read print

Learning to read is one of the primary functions of schooling to help children understand and function in their communities. Most teaching strategies use well illustrated books to carry this out. Children are then encouraged to use the pictures to find out what is in the text: 'They are therefore reading pictures before they read the print' (DEC, 1989). Reading is the *key* to educational success, so picture reading is part of that key. Several reading schemes produced in the past decade included wordless picture books as starting points and suggested ways in which adults could prompt children's responses to the visual images. The term picture book used in this context is possibly misleading, the picture books are part of a reading scheme and tend to contain pictures with very definite messages. There is little ambiguity and their commercial success as a book is dependent on the success of the scheme as a whole. It is unlikely that anyone will purchase individual picture books from the reading scheme or that they will appear in bookshops alongside other picture books. The images presented in commercial picture books are much richer and early readers need support in reading these pictures just as much as pictures in scheme books. Several other chapters in this book look at different ways in which these commercial, or trade, picture books can be used to support literacy. Interestingly the 1997 National Reading Tasks for children at the end of their infant career in England, involved the need for a very well developed understanding of pictures of winter personified. This would have been an extremely difficult task for children who had only had adult support to read a picture book as part of a reading scheme and whose cultural background precluded any real experience of British winters.

Very young children who are accustomed to 'reading pictures' in the picture books they read are often much more perceptive than adults. Each time I read an Anthony Browne book with children, I am reminded how much better they are at looking for things within the picture than I am. There is always something new for me, something that I have missed because of my obsession with the print. We have here a conflict, then, of teaching children how to read, using picture books and then of encouraging them to move away from the pictures to concentrate on the text. So children who may become good at reading pictures are then taught virtually to ignore them and concentrate on the text. In fact, older children are frequently put off by a text which has attractive pictures accompanying it and have to be 'resold' the fascinating world of the picture book. A good picture story book conveys its messages through two media – the art of illustrating and the art of writing: 'In a well-designed book in which the total format reflects the meaning of the story, both the illustration and the text must bear the burden of narrative' (Huck *et al.*, 1995).

Learning from non-fiction texts

Visual images in books continue to be important well after children become competent readers. The rapid growth of quality non-fiction texts, for example both in book and disc format, shows visual imagery used to transmit information as well as enhance presentation. It is difficult to imagine a number of different types of butterfly, for example, without the accompanying visual support. Children's and adults' ability to read and draw information from the pictures in the many attractive non-fiction texts now available influences their ability to develop the knowledge and concepts about the particular subject or theme.

Reading the page

Visual literacy is also involved in being able to 'read the page'. Children's books, particularly ones for the trade market, are often carefully designed to look attractive and inviting for the casual browser. Gaining information from the text and pictures may be much harder and involves visual literacy in a different context from a simple picture and caption book. There is plenty of evidence in our daily lives to show that this is a vital skill which some children – and indeed many adults – fail to develop to a significant level.

Anyone reading this is likely to have a reasonable degree of competence in visual literacy. They can distinguish quickly between print and picture, understand messages from symbols and be prepared to spend time looking for meaning in images where there is no printed aid. It comes as a shock therefore when we meet adults who have weak skills in visual literacy. Restaurants are one place where it is possible to see adults at varying stages of visual literacy. The starting point is often distinguishing the wine menu from the main menu, then different sections within the main menu, starters, main courses, desserts. Menus often use pictures, symbols and coloured letters to aid comprehension: a green *V* for vegetarian dishes, a brown *N* to identify products with nuts in them. Look round a restaurant and it is often easy to see people having great difficulty with the menu. Not because they cannot read the print, but because they have difficulty with the symbolism and presentation. One of the attractions of fast-food restaurants is that the menu remains the same wherever you are. There is no need to struggle for meaning within a new presentation of words, pictures and symbols.

Starting points

My first experience of the need to teach children how to 'read
pictures' was linked with learning to read the pictures in non-
fiction texts. It came when working on a local-history project
with a mixed class of 6–8-year-olds. The purpose of the lesson
was to use black-and-white photographs of Liverpool in the
Thirties to find out about what life was like. The adult–child
ratio was particularly favourable as a group of adults from a
local community college were involved and as is often true
when there is a good adult–pupil ratio, the process of children's
learning or the difficulties they encounter becomes more obvious. It rapidly became clear that many of the children were
having difficulty 'reading the pictures', despite the fact that they
were good quality and apparently 'easy to read'. In the discussion afterwards many of the adults suggested that black-and-
white photographs were not a good starting point, colour
photos may have been a better idea.

A more successful starting point seemed to be using colour
photographs of activities the children were themselves under-
taking. On Shrove Tuesday, a series of photographs were taken
of pancakes being made. The following week the jumbled
photographs were sequenced and made into a picture book with
captions. Photographs taken at different times during the day
were given the same treatment. How did children know this
picture was taken on Tuesday at morning play, rather than
Thursday at lunchtime? Pictures had to be read more closely to
prove the answers; they knew that Jane was wearing purple
bobbles in her hair on Thursday!

As a parent, one of the most enjoyable experiences is to sit
with your child on your knee and read pictures with the child.
The process can never be quite the same in school. The emotional link between adult and child is missing, for example, and
there is unlikely to be only one child in the audience. But there is
an increasing number of commercial picture books which do
encourage 'reading the pictures' and many of these can be used
very successfully with small groups of children. The emphasis
here has to be on small groups, since the discussion between
adult and child and indeed between child and child is an important one. The growth in the use of parents and non-teaching

assistants means that children can work in a small group on visual literacy as a part of their literacy time, but the use of untrained personnel has its dangers since even with good briefing notes questioning can be didactic and disinterested. Successful picture books often have more than one meaning and understanding should not be reduced to some narrow focus. Ambiguity is the warp of life and not something to be eliminated (Bateson, 1994).

Picture books designed to help visual literacy

Early visual literacy texts

There are some beautifully produced picture books for very young children which state their aim in the title: Thomas and Wanda Zacharias' *But Where is the Green Parrot?* (1972) and Taro Gomi's *Where's the Fish?* (1990). These are focused visual literacy books. They demand that children – and adults – 'reading' the book look carefully at the pictures to find specific things. Other simple 'I spy' books including classics like Janet and Allan Ahlberg's *Each Peach, Pear Plum* (1978) and *Peepo* (1983) ask the same from their readers, but it is an implicit demand and the reader needs to move beyond the title to identify the purpose of the book. These very simple picture books really need adult support if children are meeting them for the first time in school. Once children have the strategies they can work together on simple picture books and create their own 'Can you find . . .?' puzzles. Informed adult support is needed initially to help children read pictures, perhaps even more than for reading the self-evident text that many of these books supply. There are more sophisticated picture books in this genre such as Ruth Brown's *If At First You Do Not See* (1990) which involves turning the book upside down in order to 'see' the full picture and Martin Waddell and Phillipe Dupasquier's *The Great Green Mouse Disaster* (1989). This involves a careful search of the previous page as well as the current page to comprehend what is going on. All these books are fun and at different levels they enable quite old children to engage in developing their visual literacy.

Where's Wally? (Handford, 1987)
© Martin Handford (1997). Reprinted by permission of the publisher,
Walker Books Ltd., London

Illustrators whose work encourages visual literacy

Martin Handford's *Where's Wally?* books (1987) can now be bought in different sizes, as well as on a number of different topics. They are best sellers in their own right, but as an introduction to key scanning skills they are exceptional. I used them initially with whole classes of 6 and 7-year-olds, later with older primary classes and then with teacher training students and in-service teachers. Two copies of the same book can be cut up and the resulting double-page spreads laminated.

Children can work in pairs on a double-page spread to find Wally. Martin Handford provides additional lists of things to find at the back of the book. Each of these lists can be cut out and stuck (prior to laminating) at the back of the relevant picture. The strategies children and adults use for finding Wally are interesting. Most adults try a initial 'Let's see if it jumps out at me' approach and then move on to looking very systematically at the picture. They take it in small blocks and search carefully. Some move up and down the page, others move across. The interval of time between the random and the systematic approach varies considerably, with some adults spending quite some time – and a very few abandoning the task – when using the non-systematic approach. Children tend to stay for longer at the random approach method and consequently are more likely to find success at it than adults. However, they do enjoy learning the systematic scanning skills involved and several teachers have suggested the use of some form of grid reference system on an acetate sheet to encourage this.

In Graeme Base's *Animalia* (1990) the reader is asked to find 'A hidden land of beasts and birds' and also 'It's possible you might find me'. The younger reader may in fact spend the whole time looking for 'me', while the older reader can scan for the birds and beasts. This book, like Base's *The Eleventh Hour* (1988) which followed it, are good examples of picture books which require their readers to have a wide range of visual experiences in order to understand their content. The pictures provide good discussion points about how the illustrator has used specific techniques to hide things. Children can draw their own 'Find Wally' pictures. These can be compared to the type of pictures found in non-fiction texts which are designed to give information to the reader rather than hide it.

Using fictional picture books to support learning across the curriculum

Art in picture books

The illustrator as artist

'The picture storybook conveys its messages through two media, the art of illustrating and the art of writing' (Huck, 1989). Several writers including Doonan (1993), Huck *et al.* (1995) and a few included in this book, have looked at the art and artists of picture books. They suggest ways of exploring literature through art and media. At a simple level children can look at the work of an illustrator such as Shirley Hughes and make comparisons between books. Her books are particularly good for 'picking up narrative clues in pictures' (Faundez, 1997). The artists' choice of media can be examined and provides a starting point for children's own experimentation. Huck (1995) looks at different picture books where artists have used woodcuts and other similar techniques (collage, paints, pen and ink, crayon, chalk, charcoal and pencil). She also looks at the ways in which artists have used elements of design such as line, space, use of colour and perspective to convey meaning. In this way picture books can be used to support understanding of particular concepts and provide concrete and accessible exemplars of different forms of art.

Responding to art

Several picture books have supported children's – and teachers' – knowledge and understanding of art. Lucy Micklethwait's series of *I Spy* books (1992; 1993) takes famous paintings and asks readers to look for specific things in them. Depending on the specific title, these may be numbers, objects beginning with a specific letter or animals. This approach to introducing young children to the work of famous artists and craftspeople could be criticised as low level, encouraging children to stay at an accountive stage in their aesthetic understanding of art (Housen, 1987). I have found that children enjoy recognising a painting they have already seen. The process of looking carefully for an object within a painting makes the reader stop turning the pages and look closely at the art. If later they see the same painting in another context they are more likely to stop to look again than if they missed the initial experience entirely.

Katie's Picture Show by James Mayhew (1991) introduces famous works of art and links them directly with children's own experiences. Katie visits an art gallery and five famous paintings come alive for her. Four of these are actually in the National Gallery and one in the London Tate, so it is possible to follow up the story by looking at postcards of the paintings. Katie steps into the pictures, and so is involved in the present, past and possible future of the setting. Several of the paintings have historical and geographical dimensions – Constable's *Hay Wain*, the Ingres portrait of *Madame Moitessier* and Renoir's *Les Parapluies*, which older children can explore. Again this raises issues of how the development of visual literacy extends children's experiences beyond the here and now, and explores other times and places as well as challenging their imagination. Mike Dickinson's *Smudge* (1987) and Posy Simmonds' *Lulu and the Flying Babies* (1988) develop similar themes, but the pictures are all illustrations and so lack the immediacy of Mayhew's story.

Geography and history in picture books

Time and place

Helping children to understand the familiar is a vital part of education. When children first start school, themes like 'Ourselves' and 'Homes' are chosen to provide a framework for this. The introduction of other places, such as the nearest city, and other times ('when I was a baby'), require a tremendous leap of imagination if children have not experienced them directly (another locality) or do not remember experiencing them (being a baby). Both narrative and non-fiction picture books can help to bridge the gap between the here and now, the distant and past. They can also supply a wealth of visual stimuli to support key concepts about time and place.

Change

Change as a concept has several meanings. Brainstorm (Figure 7.2) a class of children and you will soon see change identified in

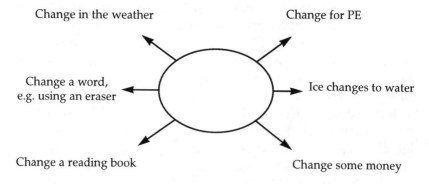

Figure 7.2 Brainstorming 'change'

most areas of the curriculum. There are several picture books which explore this concept and enable children to explore changes in both time and place. Jeannie Baker's *Window* (1988) tells a story through a series of collages which show the scene from a window over a period of twenty-four years. In the first picture a woman holding a baby looks out of the window on to a wilderness; by the time the child (a boy) is 22, the area has been built over. The view from the window shows a busy town with shops, houses, flats, traffic and people. The final picture has the son, now 24 and holding his own child, looking out of a different window on to another wilderness, which already has a warning notice 'House Blocks for Sale'. This gentle combination of change in relation to time and place can also be seen in her book *Where the Forest Meets the Sea* (1989). In this book, a boy explores a prehistoric rain forest in Australia and both he and his father wonder if it will still exist if they want to visit it in the future. The final double-page spread requires readers with highly profi-cient visual literacy skills because it shows the ghost-like pres-ence of hotels, cars, shops and people. When children discuss the spread, it is clear that the able readers understand the images created, while the less able are struggling to see the two images and can make no attempt to define what they think it means.

In both these books, the pictures invite careful scrutiny and they raise awareness and expectations of collage work as an artform. They offer images of the past and the present and ask the reader of the pictures to speculate on the future. Dyan Sheldon and Gary Blythe's *The Garden* (1993) follows this, with illustrations showing the past and present resting together. The garden, at night, becomes the scene of a Native American settlement with both present time and place slipping away. At a much easier level, Alice and Martin Provensen's *Shaker Lane* (1987) shows change in one small rural community over a period of years.

John Goodall's books – *The Story of an English Village* (1978), *The Story of a Castle* (1986), *The Story of a Farm* (1989) and *The Story of a Seaside* (1990) – are all wordless picture books which trace the history of a particular place over hundreds of years. The pictures document how time passes and changes the nature of places. Each double-page spread moves the reader nearer the present. During the course of the story, other features within the pictures change – people's clothes, their transport, their housing and their food. These books have several different levels and allow the beginning visual reader to compare the here and now with there and then, but the more experienced reader can compare there and then at different periods.

Memories

We call on children and ourselves to place the present into context. Our memories form the first pictures of a peopled past for children. Yet the concept of a memory is a difficult one to grasp. Visual support is given in Mem Fox's *Wilfred Gordon McDonald Partridge* (1984), when a young boy finds memories for an old lady. He collects a series of objects which remind him about the past and shows the objects to a very old lady to help her remember her past. The illustrations clearly show that each of the objects conjures up different memories for the boy and the old lady. The story enables teachers and pupils to explore their own memories and shows how particular artifacts can trigger reminiscences about the past. The pictures provide a visual prompt for an abstract concept, which can then be discussed by children and recorded visually by them.

Journeys

Several picture books explore this concept. Jill Murphy's *On the Way Home* (1982), Ann Jonas' *The Trek* (1985) and Satoshi Kitamura's *Lily Takes a Walk* (1987) all move children beyond their own immediate environment to explore the concept of a journey. The illustrations give a concrete meaning to the fears and anxieties about what lies behind apparently harmless walls, hedges and garage doors.

Past times and places

Several illustrators use images from the past to tell their story. Sometimes, this seems almost unconscious as in several of the Ahlberg's books. *Peepo* (1983) is probably one of the most well known of these as well as being an ideal one to use to explore visual literacy with a small group of children. The story takes place – we assume – during the war. The pictures show a 1930s/40s kitchen, backyard, living room, bedroom and park scene. These pictures by themselves produce a good opportunity to look at homes in the past. The illustrations supplement the very sanitised museum reconstructions where everything is tidy and in place. People live in Janet Ahlberg's house and the common confusions of human existence ring across the ages. The book provides frames for prediction and changing meanings. In the first double-page spread, the baby on the left-hand side of the page is looking, through the hole in the page, at the father asleep on the right-hand side. When the page is turned, the full-page illustration gives an understanding of what a 1940s bedroom would have looked like, but there are important messages for the more sophisticated reader in the photographs on the wall, the uniform on the chair and the case under the bed. This method of picture cropping can easily be replicated using photographs on blank pieces of paper, with a small card frame placed on top. *Get the Picture: Developing Visual Literacy in the Infant Classroom* (DEC, 1989) suggests many other ways in which photographs can be used to develop skills in questioning an image, using an image to tell a story, making a frame and supporting children in using a camera to create their own photographic images.

Other illustrators such as Roy Gerrard use the past to create the story and picture line for their books. *Matilda Jane* (1981) and *The Favershams* (1994) give a Victorian setting to simple stories about the past and if the books are studied together with one from a different historical period, such as *Sir Francis Drake*,

His Daring Deeds (1986), children can discuss similarities between the illustrations and ways in which the illustrator has informed himself about the past, but also kept a very distinctive style whatever the period. Older children, who are studying the Victorians or Tudors, can find visual sources for the period which the illustrator may also have used as a starting point.

Catherine Brighton has written and illustrated several pictorial biographies about famous people such as *Nijinsky* 1989) and *Mozart* (1990), but her fictional picture book *Dearest Grandmama* (1991) moves the reader on to speculate about the mysteries of the past. In this book, Maudie Ann meets up with a strange mute boy who has papers in his pocket which refer to some time in the future and a boat called the *Marie Celeste*. Brighton's pictures reflect life on a Victorian ship with plenty of detail to identify and discuss. The book is written in letter form, but the story ends with a question mark. Did the boy really exist or was he the figment of a lonely girl's imagination? The pictures provide some clues, but the final decision about the story lies with the reader.

Always Adam by Sheldon Oberman and Ted Lewin (1988) tells the history of a Jewish prayer shawl on its journey with a Jewish family fleeing Russia for a safer life in America. The shawl is passed from father to eldest son, and the eldest son is always called Adam. As Adam in the story grows older he knows that he in turn will pass both his name and the prayer shawl on to another Adam. Both the text and the illustrations hold a poignancy about communities that are forced to move and the reasons for this. In particular they show the differences between the old life and the new one, both in time and place, which text alone could not effectively communicate. There are several picture books which take the history of an artifact as their theme. *Jack's Basket* by Alison Catley (1989) looks at the way in which a children's original bed changes its use over a relatively short period of time, and Bob Graham's *The Red Woollen Blanket* (1987) shows the virtual disappearance over the years of a woollen blanket used originally to wrap a newly born baby. The essential difference between the shawl, the basket and the blanket lies in spiritual context. The shawl is linked to belief and faith, whereas the basket and blanket are associated with growing up and away from the artifacts of childhood. Blyth and Hughes (1997) explore the power of historical fiction further in their book on using written sources in primary history.

A cautionary note

There is an obvious danger in using picture books both to support skills training in visual literacy and informing subject knowledge. Both the text and the pictures can be overly exploited so that the book is destroyed as a piece of literature. The message is perhaps that care does need to be taken as to how much picture books should be used to support subject learning (including literacy) and children need to be given plenty of opportunity to explore bright, colourful and attractive books by themselves.

Bibliography

Ahlberg, A. and Ahlberg, J. (1978) *Each Peach, Pear, Plum*, London: Picture Puffins.

Ahlberg, A. and Ahlberg, J. (1983) *Peepo*, London: Picture Puffins.

Baker, J. (1988) *Window*, London: Walker Books.

Baker, J. (1989) *Where the Forest Meets the Sea*, London: Walker Books.

Bateson, M. (1994) *Peripheral Visions: Learning Along the Way*, New York: Harper Collins.

Base, G. (1988) *The Eleventh Hour*, Harmondsworth: Puffin.

Base, G. (1990) *Animalia*, Harmondsworth: Puffin.

Blyth, J. and Hughes, P. (1987) *Using Written Sources in Primary History*, London: Hodder & Stoughton.

Brighton, C. (1989) *Nijinsky*, New York: Doubleday.

Brighton, C. (1990) *Mozart*, New York: Doubleday.

Brighton, C. (1991) *Dearest Grandmama*, London: Faber and Faber.

Brown, R. (1990) *If At First You Do Not See*, London: Beaver.

Catley, A. (1989) *Jack's Basket*, London: Beaver.

DEC (1989) *Get the Picture: Developing Visual Literacy in the Infant Classroom*, Birmingham: Development Education Centre.

DfE (1993) *The Initial Training of Primary School Teachers: New Criteria for Courses. Circular 14/93*, London: DfE.

Dickinson, M. (1987) *Smudge*, London: Picture Knight.

Doonan, J. (1993) *Looking at Pictures in Picture Books*, Stroud: Thimble Press.

Faundez, A. (1997) A colourful life, *Child Education*, January.

Fox, M. (1984) *Wilfred Gordon McDonald Partridge*, Harmondsworth: Picture Puffin.

Gerrard, R. (1986) *Sir Frances Drake, His Daring Deeds*, Harmondsworth: Puffin.

Gerrard, R. (1994) *The Favershams*, Harmondsworth: Puffin.

Gerrard, R. and Gerrard, J. (1981) *Matilda Jane*, London: Victor Gollancz.

Goodall, J. (1978) *The Story of an English Village*, London: Macmillan.

Goodall, J. (1986) *The Story of a Castle*, London: André Deutsch.

Goodall, J. (1989) *The Story of a Farm*, London: André Deutsch.
Goodall, J. (1990) *The Story of the Seaside*, London: André Deutsch.
Gomi, T. (1990) *Where's the Fish?* London: Macmillan, London.
Graham, B. (1987) *The Red Woollen Blanket*, London: Walker Books.
Hampshire (1989) *Beyond the Frame: A Pack of Photographs and Activities*, Hampshire LEA.
Handford, M. (1987) *Where's Wally?*, London: Walker Books.
Housen, A. (1987) Three methods for understanding museum audiences, *Museum Studies Journal*, spring–summer.
Huck, C. *et al.* (1995) *Children's Literature in the Elementary School*, New York: Harcourt Brace.
Jonas, A. (1985) *The Trek*, London: Julia MacRae/Franklin Watts.
Kitamura, S. (1987) *Lily Takes A Walk*, London: Picture Corgi.
Maidenhead Teachers' Centre (1988) *Doing Things*, London: Trentham Books.
Mayhew, J. (1991) *Katie's Picture Show*, London: Orchard Books.
Micklethwait, L. (1992) *I Spy: An Alphabet in Art*, London: Collins.
Micklethwait, L. (1993) *I Spy: Numbers in Art*, London: Collins.
Murphy, J. (1982) *On the Way Home*, London: Macmillan.
NCC (1989) *Circular 6: The National Curriculum and Whole Curriculum Planning: Preliminary Guidance*, York: NCC.
Oberman, S. and Lewin, T. (1988) *Always Adam*, London: Victor Gollancz.
Provensen, A. and Provensen, M. (1987) *Shaker Lane*, London: Walker Books.
Sheldon, D. and Blythe, G. (1987) *The Garden*, London: Hutchinson.
Simmonds, P. (1988) *Lulu and the Flying Babies*, London: Jonathan Cape.
Waddell, M. and Dupasquier, P. (1989) *The Great Green Mouse Disaster*, London: Beaver.
Zacharias, T. and Zacharias, W. (1972) *But where is the Green Parrot?* London: Piccolo.

Chapter 8

The Beano–Dandy *phenomenon*

Geoff Fenwick

The comic is probably the most controversial artform which
children regularly encounter. Condemned as crude, superficial
and meretricious, praised for being skilfully crafted, clever and
worthwhile, it has provoked debate over a lengthy period of
time. There is little doubt that most children enjoy comics. Survey after survey has revealed this. One might consider, in this
respect, the two largest and most systematic investigations conducted in the UK. The Schools Council survey (Whitehead *et al.*,
1977) of 8,000 pupils found at the age of 10, 83% of boys and 86%
of girls read some sort of periodical, the most popular of which
were the *Beano* and *Dandy* comics. Although the compilers of
this survey had little to say that was good about comics, deplor-
ing, for example, the lack of words and the low level of language, they were in no doubt about the strength of their impact:
'In general it is evident that comics are the most potent form of
periodical reading' (*ibid.*, p. 161).

In 1996 a Children's Literature Research Centre survey using a
similarly sized sample discovered that up to the age of 7, 76% of
boys and 73% of girls regularly read comics. For pupils aged
between 7 and 11 the figures were 73% and 60% respectively.
And almost twenty years after the last big survey the *Beano* and
Dandy retained their top-ranking positions.

What might be the reasons for the long-standing popularity of
comics in general and the *Beano* and *Dandy* in particular? The

late A.S. Neill, a noted progressive amongst educationalists, and the head of Summerhill school, put his finger on one reason as long ago as 1916 (p. 28): 'Comics avoid circumlocution. The penny dreadful goes straight to the point.'

Penny dreadful, a term associated with cheap comics, was rendered obsolete long ago. Yet comics have remained value for money and the most popular tend to be the most cheap. Economy in words and price, then, might be two important factors which assist in making comics so attractive to young readers. Another is readability. Tests which measure this usually involve word and sentence length. In addition, personal words and personal sentences are sometimes used. The former consist of personal pronouns and people's names, the latter of conversational language. As the language of comics is almost always brief and personal is it any wonder that they tend to be very easy to read? The following randomly selected quotations might illustrate this: 'SQUEAL! CREEPY CRAWLIES!' 'YOU DESERVE A MEDAL FOR THIS!'

Equally important, the relationship between words and pictures is increasingly regarded as an important link in the reading process. Visual literacy, which might be seen as the ability to interpret the meaning of illustrations of various kinds, is now accepted as being part of children's early reading. This should not be surprising. Prehistoric carvings often related stories by means of pictures, the earliest form of Egyptian writing was the pictogram and the illuminated scripts written by monks were to some extent pictorial. In addition, the Bayeux tapestry has sometimes been claimed to be an early example of the strip cartoon.

For modern examples of the power of pictures in cartoon form, one need look no further than *The Snowman* and *Up and Up*, wordless stories in strip-cartoon format by Raymond Briggs (1976) and Shirley Hughes (1979), two of our foremost writer-illustrators. The pictures tell the stories on their own.

Comics for young children are often funny. Much of the humour is in the knock-about, slapstick style of the *Beano*'s 'Bash Street Kids,' the creation of Leo Baxendale, one of the most original artists ever to draw for that comic. For example, when asked to build large sandcastles, the Bash Street pupils completely surround their teacher with them so that they can escape to the shore unsupervised.

Whether funny or not, most comics are subversive in terms of adult–child relationships. Children might not always win but they certainly have fun defying adult edicts and, more often than not, have the last laugh. It is this constant challenge to grown-ups' authority, often making adult ideas seem futile, which is, perhaps, the most important factor to contribute to the combination of pictures and words which makes up a comic. For comics are nothing if not child centred.

What makes a comic a comic?

A perfectly reasonable definition of a comic might stipulate cartoons in serialised form, humour and a relatively small number of words. Comics, however, are complex and defy simple definitions. Some of them, particularly war and horror comics, are unlikely to be funny at all. Nor have pictures always been necessary. Until the advent of modern television in the 1950s forced comics to become much more pictorial, many consisted mainly of short stories in written form. Four of the best-known comics of this type were the *Rover*, the *Hotspur*, the *Adventure* and the *Wizard*. Some of their more outstanding characters such as Alf Tupper (The Tough of the Track), Wilson and the Cannonball Kid are remembered with nostalgia to this day.

The main barrier to a standard definition is the fact that there are quite obviously different kinds of comic. Frank Johnson (1976) identified a number of important categories, these being comics for preschool children, comics for juveniles and those for young adolescent boys and girls. Other categories less important and more ephemeral included those which focused on contemporary sports and/or media characters, war and horror comics and those concerned mainly with knowledge and facts. This last category is a doubtful one. There have been a number of general-knowledge publications which have adopted a pictorial approach based mainly on cartoon strips, the best being *Look and Learn* which existed for many years until its closure in 1982. History, science and literature were often portrayed in cartoon style. For all its popularity and undoubted quality it seems unlikely that children ever recognised it as a comic. It was too serious for that. Children have their own ideas about what constitutes a comic and they are not easily duped.

Categories of comic which should be examined in some detail here are those which appeal particularly to young children. Before this is done it is worth considering how comics are put together.

Creating comics – the making of a genre

Crude illustrations and a paucity of words are often used as reasons for comics being regarded as literature of inferior quality, hurriedly put together and carelessly presented. In at least one respect, such claims are correct; an element of speed is inevitable. This is because most comics are published weekly and thus require strict deadlines. Artists associated with comics might be compared with their colleagues who create strip cartoons in some of the tabloid newspapers. Clearly, there has to be a uniformity of style, so a particular illustrator will be assigned more or less permanently to one or a number of cartoons. In actual fact, the artwork in comics is not unreasonable although it tends to be compared, quite unfairly, with that in cartoon books.

Herge, the creator of Tin-Tin, Goscinny and Uderzo who produced Asterix the Gaul, the late Arthur Bestall who successfully illustrated Rupert the Bear for many years and Raymond Briggs, best known for *Father Christmas* (1973) and *The Snowman* (1976), are excellent examples of cartoon book illustrators whose work has been time-consuming. Free of rigid time constraints, it is not surprising that their work is of a superior standard. Albert Uderzo, following the death of his colleague Rene Goscinny, took nine months to create one Asterix book, and Raymond Briggs and the American artist-writer Maurice Sendak can both take up to two years to produce a single publication. (Although Sendak is not so readily identified as Briggs for using a cartoon approach, several of his books, including *Where the Wild Things Are* (1963), *In the Night Kitchen* (1971) and *We are all in the Dumps with Jack and Guy* (1993), are certainly in that style.)

Illustrators of comics can sometimes convert to work with cartoon books but the reverse seems to be less likely. Raymond Briggs produced cartoons for the *Guardian* during a brief period in the 1980s but they were certainly much inferior to the meticulous artwork of his cartoon books. Perhaps he reacted badly to the pressure of weekly deadlines.

One famous comic, now much prized by collectors, did in fact compete with cartoon books in terms of artistic quality. First published in 1950, *The Eagle* was well ahead of its immediate postwar rivals. Many of its cartoons were coloured (unusual in that time of austerity) and the illustrations were of extremely high quality. These included not only cartoons but also plans of aircraft and warships. In addition, *The Eagle* included the first commercial strip cartoon in a comic. Its hero, Tommy Walls, performed magnificent feats allegedly because of his consumption of Walls ice cream. The original illustrators, who used each other as models, were recruited from a provincial college of art. For a time it was possible to see the likeness of Dan Dare, Miss Peabody and Digby on Southport's streets. Then they were relocated to the south east and within a short time had fallen by the wayside. The strain of producing immaculate illustrations to a rigid deadline had taken its toll and *The Eagle* was never the same again (Dyer, 1982).

Some illustrators of cartoon books eventually prefer to take responsibility for the writing also. This is, however, much less likely to occur in comics; hence the constant demand for writers to produce storylines for the many cartoons which are published weekly. At first glance this might appear to be an undemanding occupation, for the number of words in a comic is never particularly high. Indeed cartoons which include too much writing are likely to irritate children.

In comics, the importance of the artist is paramount. Indeed, we have seen that the epitome of cartoon art occurs when no words whatsoever are needed. This, however, rarely happens in comics. Their meaning depends mainly on the ability of the artist to portray the sense of the plot in what is usually no more than twenty cartoon frames. The writer, who has provided the plot, has now to make the cartoon more explicit by supplying a small number of extremely well chosen words. These appear either below each cartoon frame or in speech bubbles within the actual cartoon. Wherever they are, these words help to move the plot along. In addition, both artists and writers use a form of shorthand. Artists use stereotypes. For example, teachers appear in gowns and mortarboards, the burglar has a mask, convicts wear arrow-marked overalls, Scotsmen have kilts and tam-o'-shanters and retired colonels wear sun-helmets.

Well chosen words and stereotyped images create the meaning of the plot (*Beano*, 19 July 1997)

The writer will supply explanatory notices often accompanied with directing arrows, for example, 'pongy tomatoes' or 'Beano-Town Cinema'. In these ways the meanings of cartoon strips are made more clear without using too many words. The comic strip genre, then, is by no means easy to produce. It requires both artists and writers with specific skills. No one should underestimate their talents.

The comic kaleidoscope

During the mid-1980s it was possible to find abundant evidence of comics within the categories described by Johnson (1976). For preschool children there were a number of publications with comforting titles such as *Playhour, Twinkle, Noddy* and *Postman Pat*. Usually their front pages consisted of single, coloured illustrations of media characters popular with young children, for example the eponymous Postman Pat, The Wombles and perhaps most attractive of all, Zebedee, Mr McHenry, Brian the Snail and Dylan of *The Magic Roundabout*. Often these illustrations contained pleasant little puzzles asking children to find, for example, the ten numbers concealed in the picture.

The contents of these comics were mainly cartoon strips, many of them in colour. The narrative, in upper and lower-case print, was to be found beneath each cartoon frame. The subject matter was usually domestic with, here and there, watered-down children's classic stories and fairy tales. The humour was innocent and straightforward. Pleasant rather than exciting, it would be difficult to criticise these comics apart from their tendency to be mother orientated. One suspects that by the time children had started to read they would be looking for more challenging material. These comics were more likely to be read to children than by them.

The next category, juvenile comics, almost nearly matched the general perception of what comics were really about. As such they might well have represented the heartland of the comic genre. Their titles, *Whizzer* and *Chips*, *Buster*, *Beezer*, *Wham*, *Beano* and *Dandy*, suggested a more vigorous approach than that of the comics for preschool children. The humour in the cartoon strips was of the custard-pie, slapstick variety, the action was almost continuous, the drawings somewhat crude and the colours often lurid. The narrative, in capital letters, was contained mainly in the speech bubbles. Here, the overwhelming mood was one of subversion. Mothers and fathers were not listened to very much.

Beyond the comics for juveniles, there was a gender split. For girls there was a series of comics where male characters were rarely in evidence in backgrounds such as boarding schools, skating rinks, pony clubs and tennis courts. The cartoon strips, some of them black and white, were interspersed with the occasional article on fashion. Their titles, *Mandy*, *Jinty*, *June*, *Debbie*, *Tammy* and *Bunty*, left one in no doubt as to their intended audience. For boys there were comics devoted to sport, the most famous being *Roy of the Rovers* and war comics. The latter, with titles such as *Valiant*, *Victor* and *Warlord*, were devoted almost entirely to organised male violence.

Writing in the mid-1990s, Merry (1994) detected a marked change. Despite the conflicts in the Falklands and the Gulf, which might have rejuvenated the war comics which had depended greatly on the events of World War Two, all of them had disappeared as had the comics dealing with sport. Comics for girls were fewer in number as were comics for juveniles. There was, however, a marked expansion in the number of comics for preschool children although their contents were now somewhat different.

In the late 1990s there has been yet more change with contraction in some areas and expansion in others. Sports and war comics have not returned. The girls' comics seem to be down to the long-running *Bunty*. Its best-known cartoon strip, The Four

Marys, can still be found in its pages which also include elaborate articles on fashion and the occasional feature based on photographic rather than artistic skills. Photo-cartoon strips have, in fact, been present in a number of teenage magazines for sometime. Fluidity of action is often lost when this technique is employed, probably because the photographs are either stills or simulated action shots. Real action shots, presumably, would be too expensive but their exclusion often makes the cartoons appear somewhat rigid and wooden.

Juvenile comics have also shrunk in number. Only *Beezer* and *Buster* appear to provide competition for the *Beano* and *Dandy*. These last two are now streets ahead in terms of colouring, action, humour and value for money.

Preschool comics appear to have made great strides if progress is to be judged solely by the number of publications available. At first sight, the front pages do not appear to have changed very much. There is, for example, *Thomas the Tank Engine* and *Friends*. Closer scrutiny reveals front-page statements such as 'It's fun to learn' and 'Join us now for loads to do'. There are even references to the National Curriculum! These comics, much more so than their earlier versions, are aimed at the home–school education market and their appeal seems to have expanded to young pupils as well as preschool children. They do contain some cartoons but there is little humour and a great number of activities intended to assist early language and number development as well as factual knowledge. This earnest, serious appeal has been unusual until now. Whether it will remain popular is difficult to forecast, but it certainly seems likely that it will herald the return of comics with stories as opposed to cartoon strips.

The majority of comics these days come with a free gift attached to the front covers. The comics just mentioned make use of small educational artifacts in this way, for instance a cardboard ruler or a tiny puzzle. In marked contrast, the *Beano* and the *Dandy* distribute sweets.

Comics, then, come and go with some rapidity. Categories emerge and disappear as do individual publications. Some comics will go out of print within two or three years, although some of their characters might be recycled in new publications. The exceptions to this instability are the *Beano*, the *Dandy* and, to a lesser extent, *Bunty*.

The *Beano–Dandy* phenomenon

The *Dandy* was first published in 1937, the *Beano* a year later. Both have been in continuous publication ever since, although during the war years paper shortages caused them to come out fortnightly. This probably strengthened their appeal. The eagerly awaited *Beano* was followed seven days later by the equally popular *Dandy*.

Comics have been published in Great Britain for 120 years and both these comics have existed for half of that time. *The Dandy* was 60 in 1997; *The Beano* will be 60 in 1998. Why should they be so popular?

One reason is certainly financial. Their publishers, D.C. Thomson and Co. of Dundee, have always kept their prices at a very competitive rate. Both cost 2 old pennies (2d) when first published, less than 1p in our present currency. As late as 1961 both cost 3d and in 1980 the price was as little as 7p. Today, both cost 42p, less than half as much as any other comic.

Thomsons have always had an eye for the market. *Beano* and *Dandy* annuals have been published almost from the start and have always been popular, especially as they come out at Christmas. Furthermore, a number of the characters have been exploited commercially with great success. It is impossible to go into a supermarket without finding the Dennis the Menace logo on some commodity, be it T-shirts or pizza packets, pencil cases or bubble bath. Dennis now has his own TV programme and video and, since 1976, his own fan club. Since then one and a half million members have paid a one-off fee. Desperate Dan also has a successful fan club and, like Minnie the Minx, is exploited commercially in a number of ways.

Both comics have profited by their longevity. The grandparents of today's readers will be familiar with them and will be able to recall many of the earlier characters such as Lord Snooty, Biffo the Bear, Big Eggo, Pansy Potter, Freddy the Fearless Fly, Tin Can Tommy, Hungry Horrace and Roger the Dodger. Both comics maintain a subtle balance between established cartoons and those which are relatively short lived, thus avoiding stagnation. Front-page characters have always been semi-permanent. Before Dennis and Desperate Dan began to dominate the covers of the *Beano* and the *Dandy*, their predecessors could be counted on one hand. The humour might be rough and vigorous but girl characters have never been excluded. Pansy Potter, Ding Dong Belle, Dina Mo, Keyhole Kate, Ivy the Terrible and Minnie the Minx have all held their own albeit in a far from lady-like way.

Often, these two comics will appear to be conservative in approach. Dennis has always worn a jersey with red and black hoops and black short trousers. How many 10-year-olds are dressed like that today?

On the fortieth anniversary of Dennis's first appearance in the *Beano*, changes appeared to be in order. Dennis was attired in a smart blue shell suit and fashionable trainers. He clicked his fingers in tune to the music coming from his head set. Half way through the strip he gave up and discarded his new gear for his usual clothing. Winking in conspiratorial glee, he claimed that 'a Menace never changes'. In a similar plot some years later Bash Street School was modernised as a result of an Ofsted inspection. Predictably, the Bash Street Kinds reverted to type two issues later.

Yet despite this apparently conservative approach, the *Beano* and the *Dandy* do change; often in a sensitive way. The racial propaganda of the war years is long gone and cannibals with bones through their noses have gone the same way as costumed Native Americans and Scotsmen with kilts. Dennis is no longer regularly chastised with a slipper by his father, and Gnasher no longer bites. That is not to say that these comics are unflawed. Would we want them to be? At present the publishers seem to take the easy way out in terms of the representation of ethnic minorities by ignoring them almost completely and the treatment of Dennis's arch rival Walter the Softly might verge on the homophobic. Nor for all the vigour of Minnie the Minx are females fairly represented in terms of space devoted to them or in their interaction with male characters. A 10-year-old girl summed this up admirably some time ago: 'I think', she said, 'that Dennis and Minnie should do naughty things together.' Perhaps they might by the millennium when, rest assured, the *Beano* and the *Dandy* will still be with us and taking on the opposition of staid adulthood.

Comics in education

Can comics be used in the primary classroom? One response to this question is that they are often there already. They can be found stacked up in cupboards ready to be taken out during breaks and lunchtimes when the weather is inclement and children need to be occupied. Clearly their popularity and readability can contribute to maintaining order in difficult situations.

Might it be possible to go further than this and accept that comics can assist in the teaching of reading? They are, in most cases, fine examples of visual literacy, the clear messages of the pictures being assisted by the short, readable texts.

Is it acceptable for comics to be used during silent reading sessions? There are, of course, understandable difficulties here. Teachers who allow their use often feel uneasy about it, anxiously keeping an eye on the classroom door and hoping no one will come in to question the legitimacy of their decisions. Some schools do, in fact, allow comics to be used during silent reading. In a recent investigation, Fenwick and Reader (1996) discovered that 31% of the schools in their survey allowed comics to be used in this way. This fairly low figure might well be an indication of the difficult nature of the problem. For those with doubts it might not harm to consider Jenkinson's statement (1940). Children, he claimed, read at a variety of levels. There is the residual level which they often return to, the actual one which they are comfortable with and the possible one to which they reach out. Comics seem to have a place in this far-sighted developmental approach although it would be an error to think that they are simply best suited to slow-learning readers. Moon's research (1972) indicated that better readers simply read more comics. Whatever reading level a child is at, using comics during silent reading does not seem to be a bad idea.

Comics are also ideal for comprehension work. Cartoon frames are usually sequenced and can be cut up and reassembled by children. Alternatively, the speech bubbles can be taken out and pupils asked to support their own words. In addition, the pictures and bubbles might be matched.

Comics can also be helpful in their teaching of punctuation. The contents of the bubbles are usually direct speech. Once children can master this concept they will probably have an understanding of what direct speech entails.

Another form of comprehension common to comics is the interpretation of jokes. Recent research indicates that children who are helped to work out the meaning of jokes improve their

The Secrets of Amazing Albert (Alun, 9 years old)

reading comprehension. Furthermore, when encouraged to create their own written jokes, their reading ages appear to improve (Yuill, 1996).

Children can, in addition, create their own comics, either individually or in a group. Johnson (1972) and Otty (1975) have already provided evidence in this respect. Some caution needs to be exercised here, however. We have seen that creating a comic is a complex business and few pupils will extend such work beyond six frames to any effect. Nevertheless the comic is a genre form which pupils could be encouraged to try, and when they do, they often make use of comics' conventional symbols. One avid reader of comics, for instance, happily created a strip cartoon about his school which portrayed the teachers in mortar boards and gowns despite the fact that they never wore them. Other children used speech bubbles and explanatory comments to good effect in their strip cartoon texts.

Spode (1983) and Merry (1994) have provided further examples of how children might use comics. The former requested children to forecast the possible contents of comics by means of their titles and to indicate how drawings of cartoon characters convey messages about personality and action. Spode also advocated the use of onomatopoeic words such as 'Splatt', 'Yarooo' and 'Bzzzzz' to indicate story sequence. In addition, several of these words could be placed in a cartoon frame and the children would supply the pictures. Merry thinks that older primary pupils can examine the social implications of comics. Do, for instance, adults and children really behave in a particular way? He also regards the transformation of the cartoon strip to written narrative form as a useful exercise.

There is little doubt, then, that comics can be used in the classroom in a variety of ways. There must, however, be some reservations about this. For comics are essentially for children's enjoyment and appreciation. Many adults have claimed that an enjoyment of comics set them on the road to effective reading. But if teachers commandeer comics too seriously then pupils might well be resentful and comics will be hidden under the desk to be read surreptitiously.

Comics should never be treated too earnestly, too seriously. Essentially, their humour and their illustrations are for children's delight. Their subversive element, in particularly, is allergic to well intentioned attempts to make comics respectable resources for formal education. Would *Bunty*, the *Beano* and the *Dandy* have lasted for so long had they become, to borrow a word from the late Damon Runyun, 'legitimate'? It is unlikely.

Bibliography

Briggs, R. (1973) *Father Christmas*, London: Hamish Hamilton.
Briggs, R. (1976) *The Snowman*, London: Hamish Hamilton.
Children's Literature Research Centre (1996) *Young People's Reading of the End of the Century*, London: Roehampton Institute.
Dyer, P.R. (1982) A Southport revolution – the birth of a comic, *Lancashire Life*, February, pp. 34–6.
Fenwick, G. (1992) Dennis the Menace and Minnie the Minx – a study of two popular cartoon characters. Unpublished dissertation, Open University.
Fenwick, G. and Reader, P. (1996) Sustained reading in the primary school – a survey. Unpublished paper, John Moores University.
Hughes, S. (1979) *Up and Up*, London: Bodley Head.
Jenkinson, A.J. (1940) *What do Boys and Girls Read?* London: Methuen.
Johnson, A. (1972) Comic strip co-operative, *The Times Educational Supplement*, 17 March.
Johnson, F. (1976) Anti-Superman, in Tucker, N. (ed.) *Suitable for Children – Controversies in Children's Literature*, London: Chatto & Windus.

Merry, R. (1994) Comics – motivation or menace? *Language and Learning,* September/October pp. 6–9.

Moon, C. (1972) *A Survey of the Reading of School Children,* Bristol: Teachers' Research Group, Bristol University.

Neill, A.S. (1916) *A Dominie's Log,* Herbert Jenkins.

Otty, N. (1975) Getting it together, *The Times Education Supplement,* 7 November pp. 22–3.

Sendak, M. (1963) *Where the Wild Things Are,* London: Bodley Head.

Sendak, M. (1971) *In the Night Kitchen,* London: Bodley Head.

Sendak, M. (1993) *We are all in the dumps with Jack and Guy,* New York: HarperCollins.

Spode, P. (1983) Comics – a controversial resource, *Reading,* Vol. 17, no. 2, pp. 67–86.

Whitehead, F., Capey, A.C., Maddren, W. and Wellings, A. (1977) *Children and Their Books,* London: Macmillan.

Yuill, N. (1996) in Cornoldi, C. and Oakhill, J. (eds.) *Reading Comprehension Difficulties – Processes and Intervention,* NJ Erlbaum.

Chapter 9

Now I think like an artist: responding to picture books

Cheri Anderson, Gloria Kauffman and Kathy G. Short

A small group of 7-year-old children are sharing their favourite parts of *Hansel and Gretel* in a literature circle when Pat suddenly comments, 'I think that the witch is really the stepmother in disguise'. Gloria, his teacher, looks at him with surprise and scepticism, 'What makes you think that?' Pat takes the book and carefully points to the illustrations, 'Look. The witch and the stepmother are never in the same part of the story. When the children kill the witch and go home, they find out that the step-mother has died while they were gone. And the two look a little bit alike in the pictures'. 'Yeah,' comments Harmony, 'the witch didn't even act or look like a *real* witch.' The group crowds around the picture book carefully examining the illustrations and the text to excitedly explore this new interpretation of a familiar story.

Pat's comment reminds us that reading the illustrations along with the text can dramatically change the interpretations of a book. When readers skip the illustrations, they miss a great deal of the story itself. As adults, we often become so fixated on words that we quickly skim the illustrations. Readers have to interpret both print and pictures actually to 'read' a picture book. The illustrations are not an extension of the print that only reinforce the meanings of the words, but are essential for constructing understandings of the story. We realised we had put so much emphasis on words and written language that we were not involving children in experiences that allowed them to understand the role illustrations play in picture books. We also knew that to plan these experiences we needed a strong knowledge base for how pictures create meaning.

We were aware that children are much more visually orientated than adults because they are immersed in a visual culture of television, videogames, computers and advertisements. Many adults have had the experience of reading with young children who pore over a single illustration or who notice visual details adults miss even with multiple readings of the same book. However, while children constantly use and interpret visual images, they often are unable to analyse and think critically about those images. They need to 'see' in the fullest sense and to recognise the significance of what they are seeing – to become truly visually literate in their ability to discriminate and interpret visual images critically (Considine, 1986).

As children become visually literate, they are able to communicate effectively through interpreting and creating images in a variety of visual media. We believe that picture books offer a unique potential for children to develop visual literacy because they can return to the books to explore, reflect and critique these visual images. As they explore illustrations and develop the ability to read images, they will attain deeper meanings from literature *and* an awareness of how visual images are used in their own meaning-making.

This chapter focuses on our experiences exploring visual literacy through readers' responses to picture books in two contexts. The first is a graduate course on the 'Art of the Picture Book' at the University of Arizona where teachers and librarians engaged in an inquiry on art as meaning-making. Co-taught by Cheri and Kathy, this course drew on Kathy's expertise with children's literature and reader response and Cheri's background as a visual artist and a curriculum specialist working with children and teachers. The second is a multiage classroom at Maldonado Elementary School in Tucson of 9–11-year-old children engaged in an inquiry on prejudice. Gloria, their teacher, has worked extensively with sign systems and picture books in her classroom. In both classrooms, we created learning environments where learners became visually literate through discussing picture books in literature circles and creating their own art pieces in studio.

Interpreting and composing art

Within our teaching contexts, we wanted to provide many experiences for children and adults with picture books. Because of our previous experiences with language, we knew that they needed to be both composers and interpreters of art. It has become a cliché that children learn to write by reading and to read by writing. We believe that for children and adults to be able to 'read' and interpret pictures, they also have to compose their own illustrations. If they see themselves as artists and authors, their responses to picture books are more complex because of 'insider' knowledge on how to tell stories through illustrations and words. On the other hand, their close examination and interpretation of picture books and art prints provide a more extensive repertoire of artistic strategies to pull from in their own artwork.

While *interpreting* and *composing* are both processes of constructing meaning, we use the two terms to signal the different roles taken by the learner. Interpreting art involves constructing meaning through 'reading' illustrations and artwork while composing art involves constructing meaning through 'authoring' a piece of art (Short and Kauffman, 1997).

These understandings about art as a meaning-making process are based in semiotic theories of sign systems (Peirce, 1966; Siegel, 1984). A sign system perspective defines literacy as all the ways in which people share and make meaning, including music, art, mathematics, movement, drama and language. These sign systems are tools for thinking as well as ways to communicate with others. Each sign system has a special contribution to make to human experience and a different potential for creating meaning (Eisner, 1994). Based on these understandings, we redefined 'text' to mean any chunk of meaning that has unity and can be shared with others, such as a picture book, piece of art, a dance, a mathematical equation or a song (Short, 1986).

While schools have focused almost exclusively on language, we believe that all the sign systems are *basic* processes that should be available to all learners. We do not accept the view that these sign systems are special talents possessed by only a few 'gifted' people. Although there are differences in our abilities within different systems, we all possess the potential to use these as natural ways of making and sharing meaning. We do not have to become professional artists in order to use art in our daily lives.

We feel that children's and adults' discomfort with some sign systems results from the lack of exposure to, and use of, those systems. We believe that if learners are immersed in all sign systems in the same ways they are surrounded with language throughout the day, they will be able to use these systems in powerful and meaningful ways in their lives. These beliefs about sign systems are the basis for our explorations of art as a meaning-making process involving both interpreting and composing. In the elementary classroom, children engaged in an inquiry on prejudice which grew out of their year-long interest in how the world works. Art was not their focus but a tool they used as they pursued their questions about prejudice. They read picture books and art prints to examine issues of prejudice and sketched and created art pieces to think through these issues. In the university classroom, the inquiry was on art itself and 'how pictures mean' (Bang, 1991). Students studied art as a process, but also had opportunities to use it as a tool for making meaning as they responded to picture books or created pieces of art. The experiences of children and adults with picture books as they interpreted and composed art are examined in the following sections of this chapter.

Art as a meaning-making process

The Art of the Picture Book was designed as a course for teachers and librarians to examine the role of visual literacy in understanding picture books. The course focused specifically on picture books and illustration, but our broader purpose was for educators to see art as a sign system. We worked to create the same kinds of experiences and learning environments for adults that we hoped they would bring into their classrooms.

Exploring our understandings of picture books and art

The course began with students exploring several broad questions – What is a picture book? What is art? How do art and words work together to create meaning within a picture book? We foregrounded students' own experiences and understandings before engaging in professional readings. To explore 'What is a picture book?' we talked about *Where the Wild Things Are* (Sendak, 1963) as a class and browsed many picture books. Students also engaged in hands-on art experiences with artists' tools to examine the relationship between print and illustration.

Based on these experiences, students worked in small groups to create a web of their definitions of what makes a picture book. Only then did students read how scholars in the field defined a picture book (Kiefer, 1995). We began the next class by discussing the work of scholars, comparing their work to that of students, and adding new understandings to the webs. We wanted to validate students' experiences instead of prioritising the views of experts but we also wanted to learn from experts. By reversing what typically happens in a university course and reading *after* students had engaged in experiences on a topic, they brought stronger backgrounds and interest to their reading.

In the next class session, we explored 'What is art?' To tap into students' understandings, we asked them to bring an artifact that reflected their definition of art. These were shared in small groups and then used to establish a museum display on students' definitions of art. Students also read *The Monument* (Paulson, 1991) and sketched the book's meaning to them and then met to discuss their responses in literature circles.

Studio always included a range of artists' tools and media along with open-ended suggestions to support students in further exploring the class focus. In this class session, we set up studio invitations that explored various aspects of the art world, such as sculpture, painting, drawing, weaving, collage, textiles and photography. These studio invitations included art prints and artifacts as well as materials for students to make their own creations.

These initial classes established the complex relationship we saw between interpreting and composing. Teachers came into the course expecting to look at books and interpret the illustrations. They were not expecting studio and some reacted with fear and trepidation at creating their own artwork, even though we reassured them that our focus was process, not product.

We always began class sessions with interpretation since that was more comfortable for teachers. They browsed picture books that had been organised into different text sets, conceptually related sets of ten to fifteen picture books that highlighted particular aspects of illustrations we were considering in the class session. They also met in literature circles, small groups of four to six students, to discuss and analyse a particular picture book. Sometimes the entire class would discuss the same book in small groups and then share as a whole group. At other times, students met in literature circles with each group reading a different book.

One of our concerns in these literature discussions was that students would become so involved in analysing the technical aspects of illustrations that they would not respond personally to the meaning of the book. We wanted them to connect their personal experiences, their understandings of the book and their knowledge of illustration. The following small-group discussion of *Rainbow Goblins* (Rico, 1994) was typical of the talk which occurred in these groups as students talked their way into understanding the book through 'reading' illustrations and text:

> Deb: This illustration is so peaceful. I've been in places like that where you could see the stars.
> Nojood: With the storm starting. You see? Is this wind? Are the branches this way because of the wind?
> Carmen: That does look like wind to me, but I see a little bit of movement by the ripples on the border.
> Deb: But, it really looks peaceful. I think this is sort of a mental peaceful. This one, the shadows – right away, I was thinking he makes it seem scary and ominous with the shadows on the wall. They're so evil.

In each class session, the browsing and literature circles were followed by studio invitations that built from the aspects students had examined in the picture books. During the studio time, they could play with a wide range of art materials to explore the same concepts, but through a composing process. Picture books and art prints were always available for use during studio so that students could move back and forth between composing and interpreting.

We knew that students needed more time to play at composing in a non-threatening way than we could provide within the studio in class. They needed to broaden their experiences of using art so that they could get inside the thinking processes of illustrators. Sketch journals provided this time, although students did not necessarily see them as non-threatening. They were asked to make entries outside class twice a week and then share their entries with someone informally at the beginning of the class, although they could choose not to share. We spent one studio exploring different types of entries students could make in their journals and assuring them that we would not evaluate their entries, only check whether they had made regular entries.

The journal was a place to observe and capture what was happening around them through sketches, webs and words (Robinson, 1996). The observations came from daily life, their classrooms, readings, professional experiences, studio, etc. Some students used the journal to sketch subjects of interest, such as children or flowers. Some used it to explore a particular medium, such as watercolour, or an aspect of art, such as line or colour. Others used abstract images to explore emotions. Some reproduced famous works of art or a book illustration. Still others used the journal to plan a particular project, such as quilt blocks, a classroom arrangement or their own picture book. Some students used it to refine their skills as artists and were very deliberate in their entries, while others used it for free exploration or to relax and unwind.

Examining the strategies of illustrators

These initial explorations were followed by several sessions examining the strategies of particular illustrators so that students could see the interplay between strategies and the complexity of illustrators' choices. We defined strategies as the methods used by illustrators to create meaning as they make decisions in their composing. Each illustrator develops a repertoire of methods to draw upon in particular circumstances.

In one class session, each literature circle closely examined one picture book and talked about the book's meaning and the illustrator's strategies. They then moved to studio where they reproduced an illustration from that book using the same media

Nojood's reproduction of an illustration from *Ben's Trumpet* (Isadora, 1979)

as the illustrator. This process was designed to encourage them to go 'inside the illustrator's head' and to attend closely to the media and to small details such as how colour and line were used to create a composition. They had to look much more closely than they had in their literature discussions to see very small details that they would normally have missed when only attending to the overall impact of the illustration.

The following week students met in literature circles to examine text sets of particular illustrators. They then went into studio and explored the same medium that the illustrator had used, but made their own original artwork. We also began reading professional books that introduced technical art vocabulary and concepts (Kiefer, 1995; Stewig, 1995). By this point, students felt a strong need for these concepts and were not overwhelmed by these technical aspects. Their experiences with looking at books and creating their own art had created a strong need to know what experts in the field thought.

Learning about art

Over the following weeks, we examined art elements, style, technique and book design. In each case, students engaged in professional reading and then came to class and looked at text sets set up to highlight these aspects. For example, when we studied book design, the text sets were sets of ten to fifteen picture books that highlighted unusual formats, formal and informal text placement, kinds of paper and print, borders, endpapers, front matter and pop-ups. In studio, students could use a storyboard to compose a story or lay out a book, create a double-paged spread, make multiples images for borders, explore print placement with self-stick notes, make endpapers using a range of media, explore different kinds of bookbinding and assemble their own pop-ups. For technique, we pulled books into sets that each highlighted particular media, such as watercolour or pen and ink and then students explored the same media in studio.

Many students listed the studio invitation which followed the text sets on the art elements of colour, shape, line, light and dark, texture and space as the most powerful for them. Building on

Scary picture (Carmen, adult)

Where the Wild Things Are (Sendak, 1963)
Copyright © 1963 by Maurice Sendak. Reprinted by permission of HarperCollins Publishers.

their professional reading (Bang, 1991), students created scary pictures using simple shapes cut from white, red, black and purple. These pictures were taken to the centre of the room and we gathered around them to talk about which were most effective in their use of the elements to create fear. Because the shapes were *not* glued down, we moved shapes around on a few pictures as we talked about ways to increase tension. Students then retrieved their pictures and returned to their work tables to discuss tension and make revisions.

The final part of the course focused on students' inquiry projects. Some students took the text set and studio invitations from our class and tried them out with their children. Others created and illustrated their own picture books. During this time, we revisited particular invitations according to student requests in the studio. In our class sessions, we invited local elementary teachers, such as Gloria, as guest speakers to share their experiences using picture books in their classrooms.

At our last class session, we returned to *Where the Wild Things Are* (Sendak, 1963) and asked students to examine the book in small groups and then as a whole class. The discussion of this book during our first class had been very brief. During the final class session, we had to cut off their responses after forty minutes because we had run out of time. They talked about the light source on the pages, the book planning and layout, and the use of flatness and depth in the figures. They noted how the technique for painting the water varied and got softer at points and wondered whether Sendak might have added the water last to the illustrations. They examined the use of sharp angles along with curves to communicate that the monsters were not as scary as they seemed initially.

They talked about the organisation of the pictures, particularly the rhythm that Sendak established to match the movement of the storyline. They were curious about the placement of the print on the page and how the pictures expanded and took over the page as Max moved more deeply into his fantasy adventure. They noted Sendak's use of cross-hatching and questioned whether there was a pattern to when he chose to use it in relation to what was happening in the story. They noticed the changes in the moon to signal the passage of time, the changing perspectives, the use of implied lines in the trees and parts that bled off the page. They complained about the loss of the quality of the colour in the paperback editions of the book. All these aspects of illustration were considered as they contributed to this story about imagination, fear and love.

Another indication of the growth that teachers had experienced in their responses to illustrations and thinking about art as meaning-making was found in their final self-evaluations. The following excerpt from one teacher's final self-evaluation reflects the comments that many made:

> At first, I wasn't sure exactly what I would get out of the course other than an intense exposure to children's literature. As the semester progressed, I found that I was looking at things in a different way. I am spending more time in my classroom and life delving into and discussing illustrators, illustrations, and processes. I am more curious about illustrator techniques and thoughts. I am also realising the value of creating and gaining meaning through a variety of sign systems, and noticing how different children show different strengths when they have an opportunity to express themselves in a variety of ways. I am realising how much children already read from illustrations and am hoping to nurture and further develop that ability.

Art as a tool for inquiry

While the university course focused on inquiry into art as a meaning-making process, Gloria's children were focused on an inquiry into prejudice. Within this focus, picture books and art prints extended their understandings of prejudice. These picture books and their own sketching and artwork were tools they used to examine their questions about prejudice. So although they used art for making meaning, it was not their primary focus of attention. However, our emphasis on creating opportunities both to interpret and compose meaning through art remained the same.

The children's interest in prejudice grew out of a field trip to an Anne Frank exhibit at the beginning of the year. At that point, children were exploring a wide range of topics to determine their first inquiry focus. It soon became clear that their responses to chapter books, picture books, current events and exploration centres kept returning to issues of prejudice. However, when Gloria asked children to create a web of their initial understandings of prejudice, it was evident that they saw prejudice as limited to racial tension between blacks and whites.

Exploring prejudice through interpreting picture books

Gloria was concerned about their limited perspective and put together a set of picture books that she hoped would provide many viewpoints. The set included picture books on issues of race, ethnicity, gender, physical disabilities, age and social class. Some of the books were read aloud and discussed as a whole class while others were read with a partner or in literature circles. Children examined and interpreted closely both the text and the illustrations as they talked about prejudice.

One literature circle discussed *John Brown* (Everett, 1993), a picture book set in the USA before the Civil War that told the true story of one man's attempt to free slaves which resulted in his own death by hanging. The illustrator, Jacob Lawrence, used bold, flat, elongated shapes and muted grey, blue and black tones which contrast with shaded complementary colours. Children immediately began discussing the significance of the colours in the book and their relation to prejudice:

Chela: In the beginning of the book, the end pages were red all over. I thought there was going to be death in the book.

Ramon: And also John Brown kept talking about that slavery would not end until blood is shed and the end pages are the color of blood. Also the end pages might stand for the beating when they were whipped.

Chela: As I was looking at the picture of the house burnt in like a red puddle, I thought that maybe it was a puddle of blood going down the house to stand for hatred.

Children also used the illustrations to notice details about the story which were not contained in the text itself. One group read *Baseball Saved Us* (Mochizuki, 1993), the story of a young Japanese American boy who plays baseball in an internment camp during World War Two. The illustrations look like old photographs due to the warm sepia tone and the grainy texture of the realistic images:

Ashley: It looks like all the women are the only ones that are doing the sewing.

Ramon: Men do some of that.

Michelle: It's stereotyping.

Ashley: Yeah. You can see all the men out here making the baseball stands and all women are sewing uniforms.

Children also used the illustrations to analyse characters' emotions. Renee focused on a picture where the boy is shown sitting alone in the school cafeteria at the end of the war. She recognised the significance of this picture and commented on the loneliness and discrimination the boy was experiencing because of his ethnicity. Her comment started a long discussion about the boy's loneliness. Sean noted, 'This kid's lonely and he takes all his anger out on the ball.' 'Yeah. He was just so frustrated and he knew he had to hit to prove to everybody,' added Amanda. Renee countered, 'I don't think he was trying to prove he could hit it. He was just trying to show people that he's still a person even though he's different. Look at him here. He looks brave.'

This group continuously returned to the illustrations to analyse the actions of the guard in the camp, to examine the way in which the fences imprisoned the boy and his family, to see how the illustrator used colour to make the boy stand out even though he was the smallest child in the picture, and to look closely at the faces and the gesture line of the body to determine the emotions of the characters. They even noted how the faded brown tones

Baseball Saved Us
Text copyright © 1993 by Ken Mochizuki. Illustrations copyright ©
1993 by Dom Lee. Reprinted by permission of Lee & Low Books, Inc.

of the illustrations signalled the past and history. They interwove
the print, the illustrations and their own experiences to create
complex understandings about this story and prejudice.

 Children responded to many of these books in their literature
logs. Often they composed sketches, webs and charts after reading a book as a way to think about prejudice. They also used
'Sketch to Stretch' (Short and Harste, 1996) where they created a
sketch of the meaning of the book to share with others.

 Over several days, the class read-aloud time focused on children, such as those in *White Socks Only* (Coleman, 1996), about
an African-American child who drinks from a 'whites only'
fountain, *Flowers on the Wall* (Nerlove, 1996), about a Jewish
child in hiding who paints the world she's not allowed to see
and *The Bracelet* (Uchida, 1993), about a Japanese-American child
whose memories connect her to life outside the internment
camp. After listening to these books, Michael created a 'Sketch to

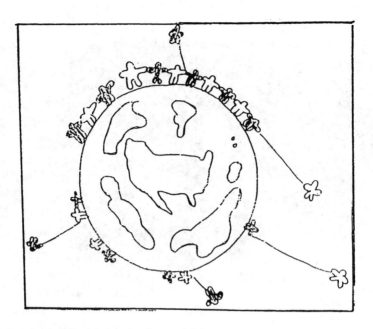

'Sketch to Stretch' (Michael, aged 11)

Stretch' and shared it with the class, saying, 'Not all people of the world believe in prejudice. The people floating do believe in prejudice. The people of the world are trying to pull the floating people in and encourage them to not believe in prejudice.'

Gloria also shared art prints as a text during the read-aloud time. She followed the same procedures as reading aloud a picture book, but instead held up a particular art print for a whole-group discussion. One print children discussed was an original lithograph by Elinor Coen entitled *Landscape*. The expressionistic muted tones of greys, blacks and browns and the repetition of intersecting lines add drama to the night scene of two children standing on a platform overlooking the city.

As they looked at the print, Richard commented that the fence on the platform 'looks like a barrier between them and the houses. They're outcasts'. Joseph picked up on his comment and stated, 'They are locked out. People don't want them because they are different'. He also noted that the dark colours in the print shut the children out from the rest of the picture. Some saw the children as locked out while others saw them as fenced in. Joseph added, 'They are living in rejection. The fence is to stop them'. The group continued talking about issues of homelessness and relationships between rich and poor.

To support their inquiries into prejudice, children also prepared to visit a photography museum to see an immigration exhibit, 'A Nation of Strangers'. A guide from the museum came to the classroom and taught children how to do visual scanning of photographs on slides. They first talked about the stories they saw on the slides and then engaged in visual scanning. They discussed point of view, pose, setting, the photographer's attitudes towards the subject, the values of the people being photographed, composition, design, content, angle, framing and light for photographs on slides from the exhibition. Because many of these poignant photographs showed discrimination in the USA, some had been banned at certain periods of time. This experience effectively combined learning about art and prejudice and influenced children's responses to picture books and the meanings they constructed from the illustrations in these books.

Exploring prejudice through composing art

These experiences also increased children's interest in art as meaning-making and so Gloria set up invitations where they could explore composing art. One invitation, 'Old Masters', included art prints that children could reproduce to get into the artists' minds and strategies. Another consisted of the abstract designs of Klee, Picasso and Dali to encourage children to try their own abstract pieces. After a whole-class experience with Molly Bang's work, children continued exploring collage and colour by looking at the designs of illustrator Michael Lacapa and making their own pieces. They also used still-life displays from the desert to create designs from nature.

Throughout this time, children participated in a weekly studio. Rather than schedule a short studio on a daily basis, Gloria scheduled an entire morning one day a week so they would have a large chunk of time for creating meaning in any sign system. Areas with tools for the different sign systems were established – a keyboard with earphones, listening centres with musical recordings, mathematical blocks and geoboards, books, writing papers and utensils, art materials and papers, and dress-up clothing and puppets. On Thursday afternoons, children created a plan for how they would organise their time the next day and listed what they planned to do and why.

They began Friday morning with a class meeting to talk about their goals for studio and then moved to the different areas of the classroom. At various points throughout the morning, children shared what they were working on with each other in small groups and the morning ended with whole-group sharing. They also wrote a written reflection on what they did and what they learned. Some children established long-term projects in a particular sign system which they worked on every Friday morning while others moved across sign systems to explore different possibilities. The sign-system tools are a permanent part of the classroom environment so they continued to use these tools throughout the week as they worked and thought together.

During the prejudice inquiry, many children pursued their own personal inquiries, such as housebuilding, roller coasters, mask-making and writing rap music. Several children explored charcoal drawings and paintings to express their emotional understandings about prejudice. The visual images they depicted came from their own experiences, picture books that had been read aloud and art prints in the room.

The children's experiences in studio influenced their responses to picture books. In discussing *John Brown*, Melissa commented, 'In this picture I noticed all the sharp edges to show how mad they are. The reason I noticed that is because once we were trying to draw our emotions and for mad, I tried to do some sharp edges'.

To pull together their understandings about prejudice, children brought in artifacts that reflected prejudice to them and shared them with the class using 'Save the Last Word for Me' (Short and Harste, 1996). Each child held up an artifact while the class talked about how they thought that artifact reflected prejudice but the child who brought the artifact remained silent until everyone else finished talking. Then that child had the 'last word' to explain what the artifact represented to him or her. Hearing multiple interpretations from others changed their understandings of their own artifacts and expanded their perspectives on prejudice. After they were shared, the artifacts were displayed as art pieces with placards in a museum. This same strategy was used with the art artifacts in the university course because of the way it illuminates interpreting as a process.

Based on these explorations, children added new insights, issues and questions to their web on prejudice. They identified areas for further inquiry including gender, class, ethnicity, religion and social outcasts and formed inquiry groups to read chapter books about these issues. They used drama to explore the issues in their books as part of their literature discussions. They then moved into a large study of civilizations and used art and drama to create a community within a new civilization. Throughout the year, art continued to be a tool they used constantly to think and to communicate as they examined questions that were significant in their lives.

Just as in the university course, children reflected on their use of art as a sign system. Melissa, age 11, wrote:

> Because of doing my own artwork, I can understand illustrations in books. I know what specific shapes and colours mean. I go through the feelings of the artist and I think about the effect that the picture has on me. I relate to the illustrations. I know I can go to them as experts when I do my artwork. I've experimented so I know what they are doing. My practice as an artist helps me understand and I start to look at what they do so I can see if I have a speciality. I think in art and language.

Reflections

We believe that in both classroom contexts it was the complex interplay of interpreting and composing that created a powerful environment for learning. When in studio, both adults and children continuously referred to picture books and art prints as they played with art materials. When they discussed books in literature circles, they sketched and webbed their responses. Their experiences as artists became important reference points for interpreting the books they were reading. Through professional readings, illustrator studies and visits to the photography museum, they gained insights into how other illustrators thought and worked. These insights into others' composing processes informed both their reading and artwork.

An important aspect of both environments was the balance between open-ended contexts where children and adults could explore interpreting and composing and specific engagements where they learned about art. The sketch journals and studio experiences where they could freely play with art immersed them as artists. These experiences created a need for learning about art through discussions, specific engagements and strategy lessons. These lessons were demonstrations of what learners *might* think about or do in their work, not models of what they *must* do. Our focus was on providing them with more options, not on imposing a particular procedure or way of thinking.

It's important to point out that we did not begin by teaching about art. We started out looking at books, talking about our interpretations and creating art. Based on these experiences, we determined the types of engagements, discussions or lessons that might support learners in deepening their understandings of art.

In both classrooms, adults and children learned about art and used art to compose and interpret because they *needed* these understandings for their inquiries. While the focus of inquiry differed in the two classrooms, adults and children were involved in questions that mattered to them as learners and used art and picture books as tools to further that inquiry. Because their questions mattered, so did their use of art and illustrations to make meaning. Art and picture books had become a way to explore and understand the world and their lives.

Bibliography

Bang, M. (1991) *Picture This: Perception and Composition*, Boston, MA: Little Brown.
Coleman, E. (1996) *White Socks Only*, Morton Grove, Ill: Albert Whitman.
Considine, D. (1986) Visual literacy and children's books: an integrated approach, *School Library Journal*, September, pp. 38–42.
Eisner, E. (1994) *Cognition and Curriculum Reconsidered*, New York: Teachers College Press.
Everett, G. (1993) *John Brown: One Man against Slavery*, New York: Rizzoli.
Isadora, R. (1979) *Ben's Trumpet*, New York: Scholastic.
Kiefer, B. (1995) *The Potential of Picture Books: From Visual Literacy to Aesthetic Understanding*, Englewood Cliffs, NJ: Merrill.
Mochizuki, K. (1993) *Baseball Saved Us*, New York: Lee and Low.
Nerlove, M. (1996) *Flowers on the Wall*, New York: Simon & Schuster.
Paulson, G. (1991) *The Monument*, New York: Dell.
Peirce, C. (1966) *Collected Papers, 1931–1958*, Cambridge, MA: Harvard University Press.
Rico, Ul. de (1994) *Rainbow Goblins*, New York: Thames & Hudson.
Robinson, G. (1996) *Sketch-books: Explore and Store*, Portsmouth, NH: Heinemann.

Sendak, M. (1963) *Where the Wild Things Are*, New York: HarperCollins.
Short, K. (1986). Literacy as a Collaborative Experience. Unpublished doctoral dissertation, Indiana University.
Short, K. and Harste, J. with Burke, C. (1996) *Creating Classrooms for Authors and Inquirers*, Portsmouth, NH: Heinemann.
Short, K. and Kauffman, G. (1997) Exploring sign systems within an inquiry curriculum. In Gallego, M. and Hollingsworth, S. (eds.) *Challenging a Single Standard: Multiple Perspectives on Literacy*, New York: Teachers College Press.
Siegel, M. (1984) Reading as Signification. Unpublished doctoral dissertation, Indiana University.
Stewig, J.W. (1995) *Looking at Picture Books*. Fort Atkinson, WI: Highsmith.
Uchida, Y. (1993) *The Bracelet*, New York: Philomel.

Chapter 10

Making picture stories: children illustrating their narrative texts

Paul Johnson

The children's picture book is not only a powerful vehicle for teaching reading but also promotes the emotional and intellectual growth of children through the language of combined words and pictures. However, this experience tends not to lead children into producing picture books themselves. This chapter argues that when children integrate narrative writing with illustration they access a dynamic form of communication.

Whereas the narrative genre is popular in teaching children to write, the same cannot be said for it in the teaching of art. What goes on in the classroom is influenced by what happens in the cultural ambience of society. For at least the last two hundred years literature has been dominated by stories – the novel – but art in this century has been essentially less concerned with producing 'stories in pictures' and instead preoccupied with experimentation. Consequently, it is not uncommon to find schoolchildren encouraged to 'explore' the tools and techniques of art and visual elements like colour and texture. Indeed, it could be argued that art as content and structure has tended to be of less importance in art education than art as exploration.

Narrative picture making in stained glass, wall paintings and carved stone filled our cathedrals in a non-literate age, and continued to influence the painting and sculpture of the Renaissance and beyond. But the subject matter of art that emerged in the twentieth century contrasts sharply with that. As Gombrich (1950) suggests, it was precisely the storytelling, literary tradition embedded in European painting and sculpture from the medieval period onwards that brought about such a reaction against it after the First World War. Art, it was argued, was not the servant of literature. It had come of age: it was a time for 'art for art's sake'. So it is not surprising that narrative themes have taken something of a back seat in the art teaching of our time.

Picture stories in the classroom

There is of course a dilemma here: children are not encouraged to make pictures that tell stories while being surrounded by them in classroom picture books. Oxford University Press heralded a new era in children's picture book publishing in the 1960s by commissioning innovative writer/illustrators like Charles Keeping, Brian Wildsmith and John Burningham. Keeping's *The Garden Shed* (1971) is a stunning reminder of the depth and range of the visual language expressed by these pioneering exponents of the genre. Today the abundance of talent and original thought manifested in the concept and design of the best of children's picture books is overwhelming. But while the picture book has become seminal to reading and cognitive development it is less common for children to combine systematically text and images in their own work.

Should children illustrate?

Graham (1990) has discussed the power of the visual images in the children's picture book to arouse and foster emotional and intellectual growth, and Baddeley and Eddershaw (1994) argue that not only do picture book illustrations deepen the reader's understanding of the issues implicit in the text but they can also help children rise to a higher level of writing. From another perspective, Bromley (1996) has described several contexts in which picture book illustrations can be used to encourage the analytical and critical awareness of children.

If combined writing and illustrating in published books widens and deepens the personal and learning development of children, and improves their writing and critical skills, then is it not unreasonable to assume that the active manipulation of both forms widens and deepens children's ability to create and communicate as well?

Can illustration be taught?

So how are children introduced to making pictures in a book-orientated narrative context? On first thought it would seem that the picture book form would itself provide the basis for learning to make illustrations, albeit at the child's own level. Bruner (1960) believed that any idea or body of knowledge can be presented in a form simple enough so that any particular learner can understand it in recognisable form. Camp (1981) makes a strong case for learner-artists acquiring drawing skills by copying the work of both old and new masters, whilst Matthews (1994) has shown that young artists can sequence pictures in a storytelling context without difficulty. But is illustration a different matter? Certainly the technical skills of professional illustrators are equal to their fine-art counterparts. Simpson (1990) argues that in both form and content there is no recognisable dividing line between fine art and illustration any more. Doonan (1993) provides a convincing argument for children studying the aesthetics of children's book illustration as exemplars of composition, drawing, colour relationships and spatial harmony.

How much of the language of illustration can be grasped by the practising young student? Styles (1996) admits that illustrators sometimes have 'complicated intentions' in their work. Regarding technique, anyone who attempts to emulate the sketchy styles of illustrators Babette Cole and Quentin Blake soon discovered that it is not as easy as it looks. Behind the rapid pen-and-brush work – the apparent casualness – lie years of devoted practice. Like writing, the ability to draw with confident ease is usually prefaced by rigorous academic training.

Children have to serve an apprenticeship in learning to draw as much as they do in learning to write. And as with writing, both technical and aesthetic elements must be mastered. Taylor (1986) articulates a common misconception in art teaching (it could equally apply to the teaching of English): it is that providing 'the basics' are taught, the teacher can stand on the sideline because 'expression' will ultimately follow. The skill to transform the prosaic into that which is engaging; the mechanical into that which is lyrical; to be able to construct art, to some extent at least, must be taught. But while there are strategies for teaching observational drawing and the acquisition of practical techniques like mixing paint or combining media, cultivating the visual imagination of children is more problematic. And besides, what is an 'imaginative visual composition'? How are people and objects juxtaposed in an illustration to make them 'interesting'? How can a dull picture become an 'exciting' one?

Illustration frames

Of course teachers of English ask similar questions when faced with the uninspired and confused texts of the young. How can children be trained to organise their written statements and expressions effectively? Wray and Lewis (1996) discuss types of writing frames as an aid to children 'scaffolding' their writing. Key words and phrases particular to a generic form – a template of starters, connections and sentence modifiers – give children a structure in which they can concentrate on what they want to say.

In the project discussed here pupils have written and illustrated a narrative and both of these have been assisted by framing strategies. It will be argued that just as children can be guided into structured writing through a prescribed framework, so they can be directed into structured picture making by using visual scaffolds. While this does not guarantee the development of clearly articulated thought, it does however provide a foundation which is more likely to produce an organised and imaginative piece of work than by allowing children 'a free hand'.

The Toy Shop project

The project under discussion was conducted with a class of mixed-ability 9-year-olds in a primary school situated in a culturally diverse part of south Manchester. Pupils had made and worked on books on previous occasions; in fact this approach to writing development was well established in their school. They had made illustrations to accompany texts, but had not been assisted in their design.

Before the practical aspects of the project got under way I showed the class three picture books and asked them which book they liked the most – what was the most exciting one for them. The books were *I Can't Sleep* by Philippe Dupasquier (1990), *Have You Seen Who's Just Moved in Next Door to Us?* by Colin McNaughton (1991) and *Who's That at the Door?* by Jonathan Allen (1992). They liked Allen's sinister wolves, and were moved by Dupasquier's lovely atmospheric water-colour washes, but it was McNaughton's colourful street scene of terraced houses and the weird and exciting people who live inside them that won the day. Why did they like it? These are some of their comments:

> There are so many people and different kinds of shops to look at, and they're all doing different things.
> Every time you look at it you see people and animals you hadn't remembered before.
> You can spend ages looking at one page and not get bored.
> I like all the detail.
> It's so funny.

Further discussion looked more deeply at the work. It was noted that some houses appeared quite normal and that this accented those houses that were abnormal – for instance, one had a dinosaur inside it. Another contrast was in the way that some houses were drawn as exteriors and others as 'X-ray' interiors. Also, in addition to the four-line stanza narrative, cartoon 'bubbles' added humorous asides to the text.

They liked this picture book because it held the eye through invention, was funny and they could identify with it – the shops and houses were, ostensibly, just like the ones in the high street next to the school. Its popularity was hardly surprising. Popular movies are 'action packed', one thrill after another, never a dull moment. The world of comics, computer games and TV in general is fast moving, instantly demanding the attention of the viewer. McNaughton produces similar excitement and action through colourful washes and lively penwork illustrations. Would these children like to make an illustrated story full of entertaining imagery like this too? This question was put to them and they immediately responded in the affirmative.

Near where Adam lived was a toy shop...

Every day Adam...

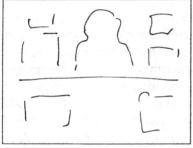

Over the counter of the toy shop was the owner, Mr/Mrs...

"Oh dear, I've broken it," said Adam. But there inside was a ...

Adam held it in his hands...

CONTINUE STORY

So they went...

Storyboard

The strategy

Making book forms

A zigzag concertina book comprising eight spreads was made for every pupil. (The pages measured 22 × 15 cm) Card templates 1 cm smaller than the landscape-orientated pages were made for each pair of pupils. They took it in turns to draw around this on the first left-side page thus providing a 1 cm margin to the page.

Designing the storyboard

A storyboard comprising six boxes with a story suggestion beneath each of them had been prepared. Each of the boxes had in them a pictorial frame. These suggested two exterior street scenes and four interior environments. Structurally, the first five frames are free from the constraints of perspectival drawing. If you look face on to a shop front the horizontal components of the facade are parallel to one another. If you then follow these 'lines' left and right down the street, the ones above eye level appear to slant downwards, and the ones below the eye level appear to slant upwards. Eventually, both lines converge at the 'vanishing point'. Vertical 'lines' (e.g. the uprights of doors and window frames) appear to get closer the further the distance from the viewer. If all doors and windows are the same size the interval of regression is precise. Drawing perspectively is then both an art and a science. While drawing in this way is an essential component of learning the art of picture making it is nevertheless demanding on the visual intelligence of children for the appearance of every object is conditioned by the spatial position of the viewer. In these illustration frames pupils are freed from the visual demands of perspectival drawing and draw as if they were looking solely forward at the scene. Doing so, they can focus on the content and composition of the subject matter.

These storyboard sheets were now distributed one to each pupil. We discussed the partly prescribed and implied story written on them: 'A boy called Adam is drawn to a toy shop because in the window is something he wants very much. He goes into the shop and holds the object in question but accidentally drops it. It breaks. Inside is . . .'

At this point pupils were invited to brainstorm possible outcomes. The last two prescribed episodes provide suggestions for this, but after box six pupils had to formulate a plot unaided. Once the class had grasped the broad theme of the story we turned to the first illustration – which would become the content of the first left page templated area of their concertina books. Pupils could see that this was a framework of a shopping street looked at head on – as if one was looking at it from the other side of the street. We looked at McNaughton's book again and saw how he might have roughed out something similar in the preparatory stages of his book. In the panel, three commercial premises had been given an equal vertical area on the picture plane and these had been subdivided into three horizontal areas too – ground floor, first floor and roof. The two main horizontal parts of the buildings contained suggestions of doors, windows and display areas.

First illustration

Pupils transferred the first storyboard framework to the first-page illustration area in light pencil. For some pupils this was not as easy as it might seem. Scaling up a pattern of lines can lead to inaccurately transferred proportions. Some lines had to be erased and redrawn – this by itself was a useful graphic exercise. It is important to stress that the framework was not intended to be a collection of outlines which pupils filled in – like a 'painting by numbers' picture. My drawing here is deliberately vague – a suggestion rather than a blueprint. The objective is that pupils visualise for themselves what these shapes are to be and realise them subjectively as artwork. The aim was to make all nine parts of the picture, ground floor, first floor and roof, as interesting as each other although, as in *Have You Seen Who's Just Moved in Next Door to Us?* not as action packed as each other. Just as pupils had described how they got the most out of focusing on areas of *Have You Seen Who's Just Moved in Next Door to Us?* and scrutinising it, so it was necessary for them to concentrate on one of the nine parts of their illustration in detail. Before this could begin it was imperative to brainstorm the subject matter.

Most city children pass groups of shops like this regularly, but the mind has to be massaged in order for familiar images to be

Lennard's first illustration

brought to the surface. So we discussed the kinds of shops and offices that could be drawn – e.g. newsagent, florist, bank. What kind of windows could be drawn (e.g. large plate glass, small paned windows)? What could be seen in and through those windows (e.g. goods for sale, price labels, posters, customers)? The task was now to select one of the shop fronts suggested by the frame, identify a specific window area and start to fill it with drawings of objects relevant to it. When pupils began either to lose interest in one particular framed component or feel that they had done justice to it, they were at liberty to work on either another window horizontally or complete the shop front in question vertically. This embraced a consideration of details like the shop design of the door – would it have a flat or a rounded top? Could there be a sign in the window? Then there were the lintels over doors and

Near where Adam lived was a toy shop.

It sold some of the best toys in the world.

windows, and most significantly the strip bearing the name of the shop or shopkeeper's name.

Gradually the nine areas were completed rather in the way one might complete a crossword puzzle for what was drawn horizontally influenced vertical decision-making. There is rhythmic variety in the design of a row of terraced shops. Each of the nine parts imposes a design logic on the illustrator. For example, drawing waving roof tiles is more reflective and less intellectually exacting than describing a shop window visually. Drawing the plant in a window of an upstairs apartment contrasts with planning the lettering on a shop door sign or large wall advertisement.

Organisationally, forty minutes was allotted to the project introduction and about two hours to each of the illustration sessions. These were spaced approximately one week apart. Before the end of the first session, however, the text for the first spread

Lennard's second illustration

had to be completed in draft and transferred to the book spread. In fact the narrative frame here can be left as it is – 'Near to where Adam lived was a toy shop', but pupils should add another descriptive sentence to this if they wished. In fact the verbal framework could be changed in any way to suit individual requirements. This tended to be the work pattern for the project over the next few weeks. At the end of the session individual books and storyboards were placed in folders and pupils were encouraged to continue working on the first illustration during free moments in the week at home.

Second illustration

The framework for the next illustration introduces the main character. He is presented in head and shoulders form on the far

Every day Adam walked past the shop and hoped he could have the train set in the window.

left. The rest of the area is divided roughly into two horizontal areas representing the front and rear shop-window display. After drawing the framework on the second left page of their books, pupils took it in turns to act as model while their partner drew them side view as the portrait head in the picture. Then pupils swapped roles. Next came a brainstorming on the theme of toys. Inevitably it started with things like teddy bears and model trains, but as the mind loosened and one penetrated deeper more unorthodox things like miniature dolls' house furniture emerged. Pupils now began the process of 'making the toy-shop window as interesting as possible'. As with the first illustration, pupils were encouraged to move freely about the illustration areas; could they contrast larger shapes like a doll with smaller ones, for example toy cars? If a particular toy was duplicated could it be changed in some way – for example, two

Lennard's third illustration

footballs each with its own patterned design or logo? Towards the end of the session attention was given to the written narrative. The second prescribed text is shorter than the first one so pupils had more to provide themselves. What is it that Adam is looking so longingly at in the window?

Third illustration

This picture is in some way the most complex of the illustration project. We are now inside the shop. The shopkeeper dominates the central area. He or she is facing both Adam as he stands in the shop doorway, and us, the audience of the picture. Below this new character is the counter filling the whole of the bottom horizontal area of the picture plane, and on each side of him or her are shelves holding merchandise. When drawing the framework,

Over the counter of the toy shop was Mr. John who owned it. One day Adam went into the shop to buy a chess set but by accident Adam knocked over a robot and it fell on the floor.

pupils were encouraged to include at least three shelves in the composition, so the merchandise in the shop window of the previous illustration was now being expanded. New concepts were discussed at the predrawing brainstorming. These included the use of labels and price tickets, and compositional variations – drawing the same object from different positions and overlapping objects. As pupils were working in a concertina book they could refer back to the previous illustration, compare both and use it as a stimulus for this more involved design.

The drawing began again with costume life drawing. Pupils took it in turns to draw each other for the portrait of the shop owner – front view this time – but were at liberty to transform the figure, e.g. give the shopkeeper a beard, experiment with unusual clothing and appendages like a watch on a chain. The text provided for the next spread – the main character dropping a toy

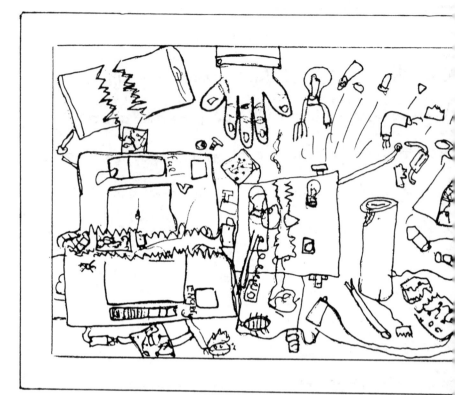

Lennard's fourth illustration

object – is a clue to what might be a central factor in this illustration and also the ending of this page's text. Pupils drafted the text accordingly, and after editing it accompanied the illustration.

Fourth illustration

Until now the illustration had been prescribed as non-perspectival front views with an emphasis on middle and foregrounds. In this illustration the viewer is looking down on the broken toy lying on the ground. A mass of scattered parts is a god-send to the illustrator for a dull area like the floor of a shop can be transformed into a galaxy of 'interesting' shapes. As the tripartite spatial divide of far (objects furthest from the viewer), middle (objects in the middle distance) and near grounds (objects close by the viewer) common to landscape and interior

"Oh dear, I've broken it," said Adam.

But there inside was a scroll.

compositions do not apply here, objects can be placed anywhere in the picture plane – we look directly at them lying on the floor. Discussion centred on what could be inside the broken toy. It was agreed that it had to be as appealing as the toy itself to keep the story alive. One pupil chose a robot, another a cat with her litter of kittens. When this had been decided pupils could either commence with the drawing, or with preparing the narrative written on the opposite page.

With the experience of the previous illustration work behind them pupils were now showing sophisticated skills of invention. 'What else can I include in this illustration?' was becoming less a question I posed and more a self-imposed question for the class as a whole.

By now it was time to explore the pencil as a mark-making object. I played a drawing game in which pupils draw a line

Lennard's fifth illustration

which wiggles its way down a sheet of A4 paper. The beginning of the line is as light as it can be made; gradually pressure
is placed on the pencil until at the bottom of the sheet the line is
a dark as it can be. The transition from light to dark should
be perfectly modulated. Then by making patterns with the
pencil, different kinds of texture and surface marks can be
explored. These techniques are then used in illustration in an
attempt to enrich the surface line work and provide textural
variations.

Fifth illustration

Empathy between pencil/pen/brush, the hand and the imagination is the goal of every illustrator whatever their age or level of
expertise. The class was beginning to feel this organic 'flow'

Adam held it in his hands.

Mr John said it was a map.

It said that Adam should go to the

back of the shop's garden.

because it was evident in their work. This penultimate illustration in the prescribed storyboard now shifted observational drawing from body head and torso to hands. The new project that was revealed here is hand held, so pupils held their pencil cases with one hand and drew their hand in this position with the other hand. (As it is difficult to draw the other posed hand with the non-drawing hand, this was drawn as a reversal of the drawn hand.) At this stage pupils' narrative illustrations began to break free of the storyboard. The new object which determines the plot development from here is on a personal matter. No two pupils visualised it in quite the same way.

The prescribed written narrative is still structured to some extent for the last entry implies that both characters move from the main part of the shop to the back of the shop. The text here, then, must relate to this development in the plot.

Lennard's sixth illustration

Sixth illustration

This last prescribed narrative frame suggests the two characters standing equal distance apart in a room. The large, vacant area in the centre at which the figures are looking implies that this should be the focus of intention. Most pupils saw this stage of the book as a challenge. They are alone now. They have left the protection of the prescribed frame and are now left to their own devices.

Outcomes

Of the class of thirty-two pupils, seventeen produced up to two more pages to complete the story, fourteen produced between two and six more pages, and one pupil produced another eight pages. The quality of imaginative and plot-development content

So they went into the back garden and saw

a rug with a picture of a scroll on it.

Adam stood on a stone which was a

trap door and the rug fell down a hole.

varied, but most of them to a greater or lesser degree maintained clearly articulated and resourceful text and illustrations. The quality of Lennard's work reproduced here was representative of about 25% of the class, while another 40% produced work that was only marginally less effective.

At the end of each session pupils shared their work with their peers grouped around the table. This was a time for reflection and celebration. As all the illustrations can be seen at once when the book is opened common strengths and weaknesses are instantly identifiable.

Some illustrations are recognisably more fascinating, hold more information or 'action' than others. But while the composition in one particular illustration is rich and detailed the quality of the drawing may be weak. This process is, in effect, a built-in visual self-appraisal. It is easy to underestimate the critical

Lennard's last double-page spread

faculties of children. When I asked individuals to define their strengths and weaknesses their views were nearly always the same as mine. The whole book is seen as a continuum. I found pupils watching their illustrations grow on the page fascinating. Some worked systematically completing one component before moving to the next, while others bounced from segment to segment in an apparently arbitrary fashion. The sense of achievement was evident and their desire to make each new illustration as exciting as the previous one became a driving force. No stimulus for getting started on their next book could have been more powerful than the book they had just finished.

Written narratives

Although developing illustration skills was the main objective of this project it was the accompanying text that gave the illustrations

So Adam went into the hole which was a tunnel. In the tunnel Adam found a Key. He walked down the tunnel and saw a door. Adam opened the door with the key and saw a toy shop with more toys then Mr Johns shop. On the desk was a notice saying: 'To Adam.'

meaning. Although words are essential in most picture books, the fewer the words the better. The writer and illustrator Shulevitz (1985) makes the point that the words selected for children's books must be to the point – there is no room for unnecessary passages; every phrase, indeed each word must have a purpose.

In this project the prescribed written narrative was sufficient to trigger the imagination – just a few words had to be added as a cadence to the episode. But that brief description tells us important information that is not conveyed by the picture. This information is essential, for not until the words established the identity of the main character and the activity on which he or she engaged can artwork fulfil its role.

From a psychological point of view the text – almost a caption – needs to be short because the eye is eager to get to work on the picture. The cartoonist, Gary Larson (1995), says that too many words on the page disrupt the visual interpretation of the visual material. In fact to compose short narrative sequences which succinctly convey the information that is required is a skill that is far from easy. It is unlikely that this class would have produced short, sharp episodes themselves without the story frame. When Lennard is left to his own devices on page nine he writes what is arguably three or four episodes on the page. Or, looked at from another angle, he has not made this episode read engagingly – we do not feel driven on to the next page, a yet unseen part of the story. Once the prescribed structure has been pulled out from underneath him, Lennard resorts to a style of writing that is not picture-book orientated. It will take projects like this to discipline his intelligence and imagination and for him to follow through a series of crafted episodes to their logical conclusion.

Visual narratives

There are many approaches to illustration, but the one developed with pupils in this project has focused on the creation of richly detailed environments as an enhancement to and amplification of the accompanying narrative text. Pupils have drawn on the mind's resource of stored images and raised them into visual reality through drawing. Illustrations made by this same class, and on a similar theme a term or so earlier than the one recorded here, but without the assistance of the visual frame-worked storyboard, are less structured and contain fewer images. Like the metal armature around which a clay or plaster sculpture is modelled the illustration frame enables complex compositions to be created. There is nothing forced about this. The viewer does not sense anything artificial about Lennard's drawings, nothing contrived. Once the framework has been comprehended and realised by the pupil as a picture it is rendered superfluous; the artwork has become the pupil's own representation.

Of course the teaching strategy here is central to the pupil's creativity. It is the carefully timed verbal exchanges, brainstorming and discussions that help the imagination to organise the composition and get to work on all those recalled images that are emerging. The skills of drawing from observation and from recalled images need the intervention of the imagination in bringing them all together in a satisfying and captivating illustration.

This raises the question of what words and pictures each do best. We have already discussed the essential naming of the character(s) in the plot, but all the objects in Lennard's second page could have been described in the text and not drawn. What the drawing does is to make it unique through the individual drawing style and vision of the artist. And personality can be reflected in art at an early age. Lennard is developing a personal style of drawing. He holds the pencil in a certain way, is learning to vary the pressure on it (learnt in part from the drawing game described here) to produce textural effects, and he brings out the illusion of three-dimensionality in his own way. This has gradually been developing since his first scribbles, in art lessons during his school career and at home. But here his progress as a visual communicator has been suddenly accelerated.

Of course writers write descriptions of things in brilliant, imaginative ways too, but it is a different kind of vision that is presented to the reader. In illustration the whole of the portrayed scene is taken in at once. The eye then journeys through the imagery, sometimes quickly, and at other times more leisurely, depending on the nature of the artwork and the circumstances in which the decoding takes place. Illustrations create an instant atmosphere. Lennard's first illustration reminds us how engrossing a street scene can be – a mass of signs, window displays, brickwork patterns. It grips us; we are absorbed by its detail. His second and third illustrations reduce the area of vision to a shop front/shop interior – we move from the general to the particular. Here again detail of another kind holds our gaze. This is also a didactic reminder of the richness of choice and the variety of packaging in the shops we experience daily and, indeed, take for granted. So Lennard is providing the reader/viewer not only with an interesting story ravishingly illustrated but also with a factual social record. Perhaps we might look more closely at the architecture, interior design and street furniture of our local shopping street after Lennard's lesson in visual awareness.

Reasons for illustrating

How can the teacher assess the significance of the learning experience in writing and illustrating projects like this one?

There is, I think no questioning of the quality of the learning experience – is there one of us who would not be thrilled if our 9-year-old child came home with a book like Lennard's? But how important is it to be an illustrator? We place high status on children learning to manipulate and control words successfully because there are so many essential uses that we put them to in both personal and professional life. Can we say the same for illustrating? I believe we can. Graphic communication is the key pin of global communication. It is said that 75% of information is communicated visually. While illustration is only one part of visual communication, in general it is a very significant one – a flick through almost any magazine or book will reveal that.

From a practical point of view the project described here has shown that it is not organisationally difficult to combine writing and illustrating, indeed the two have organically come together – each one supporting the other just as they do in the published picture story book. No elaborate rearrangement of the timetable or changing the design of the classroom was necessary. Neither would the teacher involved with similar projects need any specialist art training. All that is required is to be able to reduce composition to its essentials. Interiors offer the illustrator so much of interest whether it is a shop, a garage, Grandma's kitchen or a spaceship control room. And for using the non-perspectival method of picture making discussed here, what is required is a series of lines that suggests walls, table-tops and the like. With this kind of experience combined with other drawing skills pupils gradually acquire a firm foundation in communicating information visually. This is transferable to other visual systems like computer graphics and the Internet. If as Marum (1996) suggests, we will need multiliterate teachers who are capable of introducing children to whole new systems of language processing in the future then linked linguistic/ visual statements will become the norm of classroom practice. One might even go as far as to say that inter-related knowledge of this sort might be essential to children's survival in the next millennium. But apart from this concern, as essential as it is, what experience could be more personally rewarding for children than making their own picture book just like the ones they read?

Bibliography

Allen, J. (1992) *Who's That at the Door?* London: Orchard Books.

Baddeley, P. and Eddershaw, C. (1994) *Not so Simple Picture Books*, Stoke-on-Trent: Trentham Books.

Bromley, H. (1996) Spying on picture books with young children. In Styles, M. and Watson, V. (eds.) *Talking Pictures*, London: Hodder & Stoughton.

Bruner, J. (1960) *The Process of Education*, Cambridge, Mass.: Harvard University Press.

Camp, J. (1981) *The Drawing Book*, London: Dorling Kindersley.

Doonan, J. (1993) *Looking at Pictures in Picture Books*, South Woodchester: Thimble Press.

Dupasquier, P. (1990) *I Can't Sleep*, London: Walker Books.

Gombrich, E. (1950) *The Story of Art*, Oxford: Phaidon.

Graham, J. (1990) *Pictures on the Page*, Sheffield: NATE.

Keeping, C. (1971) *The Garden Shed*, Oxford: Oxford University Press.

Larson, G. (1995) Visual messages, *The Independent Magazine*, 24 December, pp. 21–3.

Marum, E. (1996) *Children and Books in the Modern World*, London: Falmer Press.

Matthews, J. (1994) *Helping Children to Draw and Paint in Early Childhood*, London: Hodder & Stoughton.

McNaughton, C. (1991) *Have You Seen Who's Just Moved in Next Door to Us?* London: Walker Books.

Shlevitz, U. (1985) *Writing with Pictures*, New York: Watson-Guptill.

Simpson, I. (1990) *The New Guide to Illustration*, Oxford: Phaidon.

Styles, M. (1996) Inside the tunnel: a radical kind of reading – picture books, pupils and post-modernism. In Styles, M. and Watson, V. (eds.) *Talking Pictures*, London: Hodder & Stoughton.

Taylor, R. (1986) *Education for Art*, Harlow: Longman.

Wray, D. and Lewis, M. (1996) An approach to writing non-fiction, *Reading*, Vol. 30, No. 2, pp. 7–13.

Chapter 11

The role of the author/artist:
an interview with Anthony Browne
Anthony Browne with Janet Evans

———————

Why have you always done illustrated books for children?
Well, I haven't. After leaving art college I became a medical
artist, making detailed explanatory illustrations of operations.
I used to think that this had nothing at all to do with
making children's books, but I learned a lot about the telling
of a story (the story of an operation) in images that seem
to be realistic, but in fact aren't. An operation is a mess,
and a photograph doesn't really show much information. A
medical artist cleans everything up and shows what can't actually be seen, but in a way that looks real. I suppose I'm still
doing that.

I then spent some years designing greetings cards and it was
really only by chance that I became an author and illustrator of
children's books. It was never a burning ambition of mine,
although as a child growing up in a pub, I apparently used to go
into the bar, stand on a table and tell stories to customers. My
childhood drawings were always a combination of pictures and
words, so I suppose the seeds were already there. When I produced my first book, *Through the Magic Mirror* (1976) I really
thought I was just passing through – that children's books were
just something to do until I could achieve my real desire – to be a
painter. Now though, twenty-one years and thirty books later I
can think of no better job than making children's books. Occasionally, between books, I've painted pictures just for myself,

but they're always narrative paintings and the desire to put words with the images is irresistible.

Do you see your books as being primarily for children?
Yes.

When writing do you conceive the text before the pictures or vice versa?
The conception of a book begins with the germ of an idea. At any time I have about three or four ideas sloshing around in my head and gradually one works itself to the top and forces itself out. This can emerge almost fully formed, or could just be an image – in the case of *Changes* (1990) it was the image of a boy staring at an electric kettle which was changing into a cat. I was

Changes (Browne, 1990)
© 1990 A.E.T. Browne & Partners. Reproduced by permission of the publisher Walker Books Ltd, London.

aware that in many of my previous books I'd included odd things in the background that helped to tell parts of the story, and in *Changes* I wanted these odd things to have stories of their own which could develop throughout the book, behind the main story.

So I had a start: a hard, man-made object turning into a soft, warm living creature, and the idea of lots of things changing into other things. But I didn't want it to be the sort of book where a child has some kind of fantasy and in the end it was all just a dream. I was talking to some friends one day about their daughter, Anna, who was 7. She was an only child and much loved. When her mother became pregnant they took Anna out to her favourite restaurant and at the end of the meal told her the good news. Anna was distraught and remained very upset for the rest of the confinement. When the baby was born, however, Anna suddenly changed and has since been a devoted, loving sister to her brother. So there I had it – this was the reason why the boy in *Changes* should be so obsessed with change.

I now knew how the book started – the kettle/cat – and how it ended – the bringing home of the baby. All I knew about the middle was that everything was going to change. With all my other books the first thing I do is to make a very rough story-board, thirty-two small rectangles with scribbles inside. These are like the scenes from a film, but are really neither words nor pictures. Making a picture book, for me, is not like writing a story then painting some pictures to illustrate what's going on. Nor is it a question of making some images and adding words to make the story clearer. No, it is more like planning a film, where each page is a scene that includes both words and images inextricably linked. What excites me about the next stage is working out the rhythm of the story and seeing how much is told by the pictures, how much by the words, and how much by the gap between the two.

Where *Changes* was so unusual for me was that none of this planning was able to take place – I knew the beginning, I knew the end, but I didn't know what was going to happen in between. The book had to develop as I painted each picture; I had no idea until I finished each illustration, for instance, that the kettle would change into a cat which would change into a snake which would change into a hose-pipe. This process of producing a book seemed very risky (I'd no idea how long it would be or how I would get to the end), but also very exciting.

Your books have recently been described as being 'postmodern' by Styles (1996). How do you feel about this and do you see it as a positive comment?
It sounds like a positive comment to me, but it's an aspect of my work that I don't spend much time thinking about.

Many educators use your books to teach about contemporary issues which are really pertinent to our Western modern-day society, e.g. bullying, one-parent families, loneliness, social class struggle, gender issues, etc. Are you are aware when writing your books of just how valuable they can be to educators wanting to teach personal, social and moral education and are you happy for them to be used in these ways?
If I'm to spend six months to a year working on a book I usually want it to have more than just entertainment value, in order to interest me while I'm working as much as the reader. I don't think of my books as 'issue' books, but as books that have a point to make, and these points would naturally reflect my own views, feelings and interests. If they are of some help to educators then I'm delighted that they can be used in this way.

You write polysemic picture books which can be interpreted in many different ways. What do you think about the many varied and diverse 'translations' that are made of your texts?
I deliberately make my books so that they are open to different interpretations, most of which I never hear about (probably just as well). Once a book is finished I have to let it go, like a child. What happens next is out of my control.

Some people (usually adults) state that some of your books are rather strange, bizarre and disturbing. How do you feel about these comments and any other critical, adverse reactions to your books?
I think that some of my books are rather strange and bizarre. It's true that some adults find my books disturbing, but it seems that children very rarely do. The adverse comments I sometimes

read in reviews are, I'm afraid, the ones I remember, but my reaction is mixed because they always get it wrong. All of my books have faults, but I'm always reassured in a hostile review that the reviewer hasn't spotted what's *really* wrong with the book.

Many people think that the meaning of a text lies within the author/ illustrator. However, research now tells us that it is the reader's pre-vious knowledge along with a knowledge of intertextuality that allows readers to make sense of the text. According to Barthes (1977, p. 70), 'The birth of the reader must be at the cost of the death of the Author'. What do you feel about this when both children and adults constantly ask you what your books mean?

Well, actually I'm very rarely asked what my books mean. But if I am asked then I much prefer to turn the question back towards the child – 'What do *you* think it means?' I've had some fascinating answers. I love to hear how readers make sense of my books, and was angry and disappointed when the US publishers of *Changes* insisted on explaining to the reader what had happened at the end of the book. The story ends with a picture of Joseph sitting on a sofa, holding the baby, with his father and mother on either side. The British text reads: '. . . this is your sister.' American children are presumably deemed by the publisher not to be able to work things out for themselves. The US text reads: 'This is your sister.' Joseph smiled. *This is what his father had meant.'*

Your latest book Voices in the Park *(1998) is based on one of your other very successful books,* A Walk in the Park *(1977). Why did you decide to expand on the original as opposed to writing a different book altogether?*

A Walk in the Park was the second book I published, twenty years ago, and whilst I have always liked the story I felt that the illustrations look rushed and clumsy. I've often wished that I could revisit the book and just do the illustrations again. But I think that this would bore me, and even though I think that I'm technically better now, perhaps the original pictures are right for the original text?

I've also wanted for some time to write a book from the point of view of different characters in a story. I like the idea of

A Walk in the Park (Browne, 1977) – cover illustration

showing that the world looks very different from inside someone else's head. At some stage (probably very early in the morning when I couldn't sleep) I must have brought these two ideas
together and out of them came *Voices in the Park*.

*Could you tell us about some of the thought processes behind the story
in your latest book?*
The original, *A Walk in the Park*, is a very simple story of Mrs
Smythe and her son, Charles, who take their dog, Victoria,
to the park. At the same time Mr Smith and his daughter,
Smudge, take their dog, Albert, to the park. The dogs immediately play together and weave their way throughout the pages

Voices in the Park – 'Walking home'
Illustrations © Anthony Browne. Reprinted from Anthony Browne
(1998) *Voices in the Park*, by arrangement with Transworld Publishers
Ltd.

of the book. Mrs Smythe and Charles sit at one end of a bench,
Mr Smith and Smudge sit at the other end all ignoring each
other. As they see the dogs playing happily together, Charles
and Smudge gradually edge towards each other and slowly
start to play together on the swings and climbing frame. They
take off their coats and finally dance on the bandstand along
with the dogs. Charles picks a flower and gives it to Smudge
and at that moment they are abruptly separated by their
parents and taken home.

I decided to divide the new book into four parts, starting with the woman's voice, and she tells us her version of events. She hardly seems to notice her son until some time after he disappears, and speaks to her dog with much more tenderness than to her son. I set this first section in the autumn; as they walk home in silence a tree burns, and a trail of leaves is left in their wake.

The second voice is that of the man, and this section is shown in winter. The colours are dark and oppressive and the park is bleak and cold. He looks through the paper for a job, and he also is so wrapped up in his own problems that he doesn't really

Voices in the Park – 'Walking to the park'
Illustrations © Anthony Browne. Reprinted from Anthony Browne (1998) *Voices in the Park*, by arrangement with Transworld Publishers Ltd.

notice what his child is doing. On their way home they pass the same dreary place and figures we had seen earlier, but this time his daughter is chatting merrily to him and lighting up the scene. In the background we see some early signs of spring.

For the third voice we hear and see the boy's world. At the beginning of this section I've used a tight, cross-hatched style to show the repressed, mother-dominated child. Gradually we see

THIRD VOICE

I was at home on my own again.
It's so boring. Then Mummy said
that it was time for our walk.

Voices in the Park – 'Boy looks through window'
Illustrations © Anthony Browne. Reprinted from Anthony Browne (1998) *Voices in the Park*, by arrangement with Transworld Publishers Ltd.

the spring develop as he meets the girl, the pen line disappears and the colours become warmer and brighter.

FOURTH VOICE

Dad had been really fed up, so I was pleased when he said we could take Albert to the park.

Voices in the Park – 'Walking into park'
Illustrations © Anthony Browne. Reprinted from Anthony Browne (1998) *Voices in the Park*, by arrangement with Transworld Publishers Ltd.

Finally we hear from the girl, and now it seems to be perpetually summer. Her world is bright and lively and imaginative – very bizarre things happen here. With each voice I've tried to use a slightly different painting style and a type-face that reflects each character.

How long did it take you to create your latest book from conception to the finished, ready-to-send product?
Much longer than I had anticipated, and much longer than usual. My mood seemed to depend on the season I was painting.

For the first part, actually working in the autumn, I was fine; I loved working in the rich autumnal colours, and rather enjoyed poking gentle fun at the boy's mother. But throughout the dark winter section (again painted in the appropriate season), I became depressed and lost confidence in the whole project.

or a ballet dancer... Willy dreams.

I had another book in mind which I was really looking forward to working on. This was another book featuring Willy, a chimpanzee who has appeared in four other titles of mine. For some time I've been wanting to do a book about dreams, and

I've also been wanting to do a book which is a series of paintings. Joining these two ideas together with Willy seemed like a perfect combination, and the temptation to work on this was so strong that I put *Voices in the Park* away in a drawer and leapt straight into *Willy the Dreamer* (1997). This proved to be a delightful experience and was the most enjoyable book I've ever done. It begins with Willy, holding a banana, dropping off to sleep in an armchair. The book is a series of his dreams . . . 'sometimes Willy dreams that he's a film-star, or a singer . . . a Sumo-wrestler, or a ballet dancer'.

It's a celebration of dreams, of the imagination, of bananas and of some of my favourite surrealist paintings. It was a great release to work on this book, partly because it has no plot – each picture is there because I *wanted* to paint it, none of them have to link one part of a story to another. I don't know if the book's any good, but I *loved* doing it.

Afterwards I returned to *Voices in the Park* and by then a year had passed, spring had come (in actuality and in the story) and my confidence and enthusiasm had returned. Something still wasn't quite right, however, and one day I found myself doodling with one of the finished illustrations. I started painting over one of the faces and it turned into a gorilla. I had a mixture of feelings – I didn't want to do another gorilla book, it didn't seem necessary or relevant to the story to make them gorillas – but it worked. Suddenly the illustration was lifted; it became more child-friendly, less worthy. I changed the other characters and it worked for them too. In a peculiar kind of way it made them more real, more human. And it made the whole book funnier. I was very reluctant to tell my publishers, so I took the pictures to London with great trepidation. But they felt exactly the same way as I did. I was delighted. I still haven't worked out why it works, and in a way I don't want to, but it does show that quite often the best decisions I make are more to do with instinct than intellect. So to answer your question the book has taken two years, although the actual work just a year.

How do you see your work progressing in the future?
I don't know. I'm still excited at the prospect of doing more picture books, I'd like to have another go at a long text, maybe a book of fairy tales when I feel ready, books for younger children

– it's impossible to say. It feels as if I don't have any control of what I do next, the idea seems to choose me.

It becomes more and more difficult to just concentrate on the books as British children's book publishing goes through such difficult times. It's trying to come to terms with the worst recession it's ever experienced. Sales have plummeted for many reasons, not least because of the disastrous cuts in school and library budgets, and this is bound to have an effect on authors and illustrators and the books they do. I'll try not to let it affect me or my books (too much).

Bibliography

Barthes, R. (1977) *Image, Music, Text*, London: Fontana.

Browne, A. (1976) *Through the Magic Mirror*, London: Hamish Hamilton.

Browne, A. (1977) *A Walk in the Park*, London: Hamish Hamiliton.

Browne, A. (1990) *Changes*, London: Julia MacRae.

Browne, A. (1997) *Willie the Dreamer*, London: Walker Books.

Browne, A. (1998) *Voices in the Park*, London: Transworld.

Styles, M. (1996) Inside the tunnel: a radical kind of reading – picture books, pupils and post-modernism. In Watson, V. and Styles, M. (eds.) *Talking Pictures*, London: Hodder & Stoughton.

Index